WITHDRAWN

TRUST FOR ALL TIME

THE CLEVELAND FOUNDATION

PIONEER COMMUNITY TRUST

Frederick Harris Goff

Trust for All Time

THE STORY OF THE CLEVELAND FOUNDATION

AND THE COMMUNITY TRUST MOVEMENT

By NATHANIEL R. HOWARD

THE CLEVELAND FOUNDATION

Cleveland, Ohio

1963

A FOREWORD

THIS BOOK is published by the Cleveland Foundation in its fiftieth year to take note of this anniversary of the first and oldest community trust in the Western world.

In considerable part, it is this Foundation's history since its creation in 1914 by Frederick Harris Goff and the Cleveland Trust Company. But the book also has attempted to depict the growth of community trusts over the United States and Canada and the parallel steady application of this pioneer idea in philanthropy to an impressively expanding social conservation practice.

Short of an encyclopedia, it would hardly be possible to relate the ever human, absorbing — sometimes exciting — narrative of beginnings and progress of all the community foundations. Only a few of these stories are reported here but perhaps they are sufficient to give the reader a glimpse of the enthusiasm and inspiration with which all originated and grew; of the energies with which they are promoted today, of the care with which they are guided, and of the quite amazing total of humanitarian good which they generate as *raison d'être*.

The original term "community trust" is today used interchangeably with "community foundation." As envisioned by Frederick Goff, it provides an efficient means for a person of good will who achieves success in a community to leave something behind for the community's benefit. The foundations offer guardianship of these funds and perpetual wisdom for their future administration.

Funds of a foundation consist of many large and small gifts left at different times by all manner of donors for varied charity, welfare, civic, educational, or other generous public intention. Each fund carries the donor's name or one which he assigns to it. Funds come to the foundations, generally through trustee bank trust operations and attorneys, without any campaigning or direct solicitation, but from the spread of information to potential donors as to how the foundation can preserve their intent against the irresistibility of change as the years pass.

The "classic" or original pattern of the community trust provides that funds be invested by the trustees of the foundation — one, or in most cases, several, of the community's leading banks. As a rule every donor sets up his fund in one of the trustee institutions. The trustee turns over its income (in some instances of express purpose, its principal) for the foundation's disbursement. In more recent years, community foundations have incorporated under the non-profit statutes of the several states.

The available funds are regularly disbursed by a Distribution or Executive Committee of widely known community leaders. A majority of the Committee is appointed for fixed terms of service by public officials and, for a minority of the Committee, by the trustee bank or banks. The Committee allocates income in accordance with the donor's preference as long as the purpose exists; and for purposes selected by the Committee for all undesignated funds.

Almost all foundations disburse their funds to local institutions and agencies working for advancement of health, social welfare, education, religion, culture, or community betterment.

These Committees serve without compensation. In their power are the decisions as to when instructions by donors have become impossible, unnecessary, or undesirable, and the transfer of these disbursements to the nearest rational purpose for public welfare without recourse to decision of a court of law. Trusts and funds of limited purpose which become outmoded with the changing times are known as unfortunate examples of "The Dead Hand." The community foundation, through its Distribution Committee, provides a "living hand" to keep forever fresh and useful philanthropic funds in the spirit of the original gift.

The fifty years have admirably tested the merits of each of these features of community trust operation. These years have provided extraordinary realization of the hopes expressed by Mr. Goff in a speech delivered in 1919: "Time will be required to determine the value and usefulness of community trusts. I am hopeful they will be found helpful in avoiding the evil effects of the 'Dead Hand' and in stimulating and safeguarding gifts to charity."

ACKNOWLEDGMENTS

THE ASSISTANCE of Mrs. Wilmer Shields Rich, Executive Director of the National Council on Community Foundations, Inc., in obtaining historical data from a number of the community foundations throughout the United States and Canada is gratefully acknowledged. Without the cooperation of these foundations, particularly some of the larger ones, this book would have been limited in scope.

The author acknowledges with special appreciation the reminiscences of I. F. Freiberger, retired chairman of the board of the Cleveland Trust Company, Ralph Hayes and Raymond Moley. They contributed much of fact and philosophy to the story of the early days of the Cleveland Foundation.

As might be expected, a major source of reference material for this volume was the Cleveland Foundation Library, the Foundation's files and its scrapbooks. A comprehensive study of the Foundation undertaken in 1950 by A. W. Marten, vice president of the Cleveland Trust Company, was also found very helpful.

As a final acknowledgment, appreciation is expressed to the trustees of the Leonard C. Hanna, Jr. Fund. In 1961 they provided the Foundation with its Leonard C. Hanna, Jr. Cleveland Foundation Special Purpose Fund, income from which makes it possible to publish this account of the origin and growth of community foundations.

CONTENTS

TRUST FOR ALL TIME

CHAPTER I

An Everlasting Concept

MORE THAN FIFTY years ago, Frederick Harris Goff, in Cleveland, thought through an idea for perpetual protection of capital funds directed into philanthropy.

Goff was a slight, handsome man of normally serious expression — serious enough on top of his repute as a lawyer to cause many friends to address him as "Judge" though he never was a judge. He was born in Illinois, brought to Cleveland as a boy; he was a prize-winning graduate of Cleveland's first high school, Central, when high schools were new in America. He was among the top students at the law school of the University of Michigan. He landed a youngster's berth, in the 1880's, in the Cleveland law firm which had the celebrated status of being John D. Rockefeller's counsel.

By the early 1900's, the four partners of this firm of Kline, Carr, Tolles & Goff were estimated to have individual earnings of $100,000 a year or more. They were consulted and employed by the pretentious law firms of New York, Chicago, and elsewhere. Goff could have lasted out career and old age in leisurely satisfaction, comfort and wealth. He wanted something more out of life which would, under his personal standards, fulfill existence beyond the careful operation of a successful law office. This impulse first led him into civic adventure.

He had a pleasant lake shore home in the eastern suburb of Glenville, where he frequently raised a voice for constructive good and gave free legal advice at town council meetings.

Glenville in those days was a famous horse race park on the Grand Circuit, where gentlemen breeders of horseflesh gathered to run and to bet and at sundown to relive the day's races at the Roadside Club. It was inevitable that Glenville would come to a choice whether to grow into a model Cleveland lakeside suburb or a way station for trotting racers. Sympathizers on both sides asked Fred Goff to become mayor.

To both he said: "If you elect me mayor, I will stop the horse races. I do not believe they do Glenville any good."

He was elected and he stopped the horse racing. To a few anguished members of his clubs, he said: "But I told you what I would do if you elected me." Within a few years, the Roadside Club died of malnutrition, and Glenville was annexed, at Mr. Goff's recommendation, to the city of Cleveland and immediately became the most rapidly growing residential area of all Cleveland.

These were the years in which Cleveland's celebrated Mayor Tom L. Johnson, a capitalist turned radical "boss" political leader, was leading a municipal government which his hilarious followers called democratic and the conservative investors of the community socialistic. All because of Mayor Johnson's seven years' war, fought over lapsing franchises, on the street car company because it rejected the 3-cent car fare he set as "the people's fair fare." In 1907, he drove the company into bankruptcy after setting up his own municipal lines, through friends, to operate at 3-cent fare. In less than a year, the Johnson company also went broke, and into the federal court went both traction systems. For the two, Federal Judge Robert Tayler named Mayor Johnson and Fred Goff as receivers to work out one satisfactory system.

Goff became the only "representative of vested interests" for whom Johnson developed a real affection. At their first conference the mayor, scarred from seven years of bitterest public in-fighting, was totally disarmed when Mr. Goff said: "I think we can work out something which will insure the best and cheapest street car service for the people, which will pay its way. I do not believe your program has been completely sound, but it is not entirely wrong, either."

Their result became known as the "Tayler Grant," for a long time held up as a model for economic and non-political city traction operating. In effect, the city government took control of the car lines, then leased these back to a successor private company to operate; the city guaranteeing to the company, by sliding scale fare, a 6 percent return. The plan lasted successfully for more than thirty years, by which time circumstances beyond corporate or political control plunged the system into difficulty and the city by stock purchase took over the whole operation. Johnson, who died in 1911, did not live to see 3-cent fare, but Goff did, in the second decade of the twentieth century.

So by 1908 Fred Goff had become a widely known citizen; that year, the directors of the Cleveland Trust Company invited him to become its first full-time president. Cleveland Trust already had a vague reputation then of being "the people's bank," but it was far from the institution of today, the largest bank in the state of Ohio. It was one of many not very large financial institutions, the vicissitudes and combinations of which subsequently produced the fewer larger banks of today.

Mr. Goff accepted the offer in the faith that a bank could be something more than the banks of that time tried to be. The panic of 1907 may have guided some of his ideas. He laid down several stipulations; the bank directors accepted them; and in a short time the new president had installed such progressive new rules as no loans to directors, continuous daily audit, and new public safeguards for assets. It was evident from his giving up a law partnership paying him $100,000 a year and the freedom of a lawyer's life for a $25,000 salary and the confining regimen of bank managing that he was impelled by some sort of practical idealism.

During his fifteen years as president, the Cleveland Trust Company rapidly grew into an agency of new ideas and new services, and the momentum of new goals helped it to launch the Cleveland Foundation in 1914.

The Foundation idea probably was in Goff's thoughts before he became a banker. One evidence is that he introduced, in the bank, "living trusts" for possessors of wealth who need not wait for death to establish post-mortem financial and purposeful futures. His trust department was arranging these for clients before eastern banks made any or much use of the "living trust." One of these early living trusts precipitated a fortunate event for the subsequent Cleveland Foundation. This was a trust created for Thomas H. White, industrialist, by which, after a generation of income to his heirs, he designated a number of philanthropies for eventual disposition.

Following his death ten months after he had instituted the trust, his heirs filed suit to dissolve it and establish inheritance. They attacked on the grounds that the trust was no more than a will, subject to probate laws preventing bequests to charity less than a year before death; and that the designations raised questions of competence of the maker of the trust.

The heirs won in the trial court and invited the bank to drop its defense of the instrument. The answer was: "Not while it was humanly possible to carry out the intentions of the trust client." In the Ohio Supreme Court, the bank trust department won on all points, clearing two legal principles vital to any public foundation.

During his law practice, Mr. Goff had drawn many wills — may have wondered as he did so about the ultimate fate of some of the benefactions. He certainly knew of cases of bequests robbed of their original purposes as years rolled by. As partner of a "Rockefeller law firm" he would have been informed of and interested in the establishment of the first John D. Rockefeller foundations, pioneers of the private philanthropic trusts; and he read and discussed frequently a book of Sir Arthur Hobhouse's speeches published in 1880 in London, "The Dead Hand." It was pencilled with his notes and abstracts. There is pencilling along this Hobhouse quotation:

"The grip of the dead hand shall be shaken off absolutely and finally; in other words, that there shall always be a living and reasonable owner of property, to manage it according to the wants of mankind. This again must be a public tribunal charged with the duty of adjusting to new objects all foundations which have become pernicious and useless."

Hobhouse used such other phrases as "the deadly superstition of blind obedience to the demands of the dead" — "property requires a living hand" — "no human being, however wise and good, is able to foresee the special needs of society even for one or two generations."

Goff knew as a lawyer about long litigation in New York state to divert an estate set up to turn a bell-tower into a library long after the tower could not accommodate another book. He knew and talked about Benjamin Franklin's post-mortem follies; from bequests of comparatively huge funds for loans to "respectable apprentices," even more huge and frustratingly restricted long after apprentices disappeared from American society, and of a fund to protect forever a stream that was colonial Philadelphia's water supply, which stream disappeared as the city grew metropolitan. He knew of the famous Mullanphy fund in St. Louis to aid westward pioneers (finally committed, after four decades of court interpretation, to funds of the Travelers Aid Society).

Friends today remember Mr. Goff's abstraction with the "dead hand" and his statistics of the current millions of dollars and pounds sterling within its grasp. He talked about it to bankers, lawyers, public and businessmen. He discussed it so frequently at the dinner table to family and friends that an evening was reported by Mrs. Goff when a small daughter was afraid to go up a dimly lighted staircase because "the dead hand would reach out and grab her." Riding to work mornings, sitting up front, he talked about the benefits of a community foundation with his chauffeur and sometimes received a good idea from the chauffeur. (Incidentally, Mr. Goff was chary of being seen riding to work in too much style and always left his auto at E. 40th and Euclid and took the street car the rest of the way to the bank).

To one of these conversations he was obliged for the distinctive "public" feature of the design, according to a story first told to one of the Foundation directors later by Peter Witt, a devoted political lieutenant of Mayor Johnson who admired Goff because he had dealt fairly in the traction settlement. Mr. Goff had discussed his foundation concept with Earle E. Martin, editor of the

Cleveland Press, who was interested and recounted the conversation to the *Press* editorial writer. This journalist, who left Cleveland a few years later for an eastern post, liked the foundation idea and purpose but proposed that its directing committee be chosen by vote of the citizens of Cleveland, to insure its public auspices.

Martin got from him a memorandum of his suggestion and sent it to Goff. The suggestion fell flat with Goff; what he had seen of elected city politicians made him distrust them. But he mentioned the matter at the dinner table to his wife and some friends, adding his crisp verdict that he wanted no politicians involved in a public-purpose trust.

"I think there is something to say for the suggestion," interjected Mrs. Goff. "I believe I see what this newspaper man is thinking of, that a foundation controlled by bankers or the men bankers would appoint might get a very cautious reception by most people."

Her husband fired back, but someone sided with Mrs. Goff's viewpoint. No verbatim exists of that argument, but it started Mr. Goff's contemplation of a "public" connection with what he had in mind. He pursued the issue with many more people, and out of this came the feature of the Cleveland Foundation which attracted most attention when it was born — the distribution and selection of purposes for Foundation funds by a term-appointed committee of which a majority would be chosen by public officials.

In fifty years, the occasion never has arisen to discuss any change in the selection system for the Cleveland

Foundation Distribution Committee of five, or of the public officials who name the three "public" members. These are the senior judge of the United States District Court in Cleveland, the senior probate judge of the county, and the mayor of Cleveland. The two others of the committee are chosen by "the bankers" — the Cleveland Trust Company when it was alone participating in the Foundation operation, the jointly trustee institutions as the multiple bank trusteeship developed.

This "public" aspect proved a ten-strike for popular interest. It set the Cleveland Foundation on another plane from the existing private foundations whose direction and control were perpetuated in private hands.

Further recognition of the new foundation's responsibility to the public was apparent in the provision for an annual audit of all foundation transactions. Publication in two newspapers of largest circulation of this audit was to be required, to give in detail investments, income, disbursements and expenses of the distribution committee and the trustee bank. The foresight of this provision for public reporting is especially apparent today.

Mr. Goff never believed or assumed that the community trust must mean instantaneous philanthropy, but that the first obligation on the creator of a private estate was to preserve and protect his family. The foundation's function was to be an ultimate operation after widows and children were cared for, whatever length of time this entailed. He carried out this purpose in his own personal trust, as did others in his and Mrs. Goff's family circle.

/ 9

The foundation design was clear in Mr. Goff's mind at least a year before it was implemented. He spent weeks and months reading, noting, consulting on laws surrounding trusts, foundations, bequests, intent, probate and surrogate practices. In Foundation files are detailed letters of opinion from John G. White, who was in that day perhaps the oldest and most respected lawyer in Cleveland; J. M. Henderson, counsel for the Cleveland Trust Company in various important matters; Raymond T. Sawyer, general counsel of the bank; and Sheldon Tolles, Mr. Goff's erstwhile law partner.

These opinions were to the point of giving the controlling committee of the Foundation the greatest possible authority for supervision and disbursement. These lawyers addressed themselves with all their wisdom to legal problems surrounding authority. They endorsed the Goff program to put no limitations, if possible, on the committee's decisions and choices. Dry and obscure as these legalistic letters read today, they and Mr. Goff's own comprehension of the law constitute one of the most significant stones of the original edifice. A man of equal understanding and sincerity, who was not an excellent lawyer, might not have been able to get the Foundation "off the ground" as Goff did.

His long friendship with the Rockefeller organizations led him to conversations with its principals about the Rockefeller Foundation, just then setting out into its gigantic studies of health and education. At the Cleveland Trust Company, Mr. Sawyer, A. R. Horr, vice president then in charge of the trust department; and

I. F. Freiberger, trust officer, later chairman of the bank, were his principal aides in envisioning and setting down "charter" aspects of the foundation. The actual draft was done or directed by Goff. It went to the lawyer consultants for their approval. On January 2, 1914, President Goff took it to the Board of Directors of the Cleveland Trust Company and the board adopted a resolution and a declaration of trust which brought the Cleveland Foundation into being.

The purpose is stated in the first sentence of the resolution:

"With a view to securing greater uniformity of purpose, powers and duties of administration in the management and control of property given, devised and bequeathed for charitable purposes, the Board of Directors of The Cleveland Trust Company agrees to accept of such gifts, devises and bequests as Trustee for the uses, purposes and with the powers and duties hereinafter set forth, all property so held to be known as constituting The Cleveland Foundation, and to be administered, managed and dealt with, save as hereinafter provided, as a single trust."

The Board resolved that "such income . . . shall be available for assisting charitable and educational institutions whether supported by private donations or public taxation, for promoting education, scientific research, for care of the sick, aged or helpless, to improve living conditions or to provide recreation for all classes, and for such other charitable purposes as will best make for the mental, moral and physical improvement of the inhabitants of the City of Cleveland as now or hereafter constituted, regardless of race, color or creed, according to the discretion of a majority in number of a committee to be constituted as hereinafter provided . . ."

For a variety of reasons, Cleveland Trust was the sole trustee and manager of the fund. A realistic reason was the attitude of other banks and bankers, most of whom regarded Mr. Goff's invention as chimerical, a plunge into uncharted philanthropic waters, or a shrewd competitive money-making scheme. Several respected bankers and lawyers privately committed themselves to such terms as "newfangled," "over-idealistic," and "tricky." In this situation, the pioneer community trust of the United States lost its chance to be first to establish the modern multiple trusteeship.

It might be assumed that President Goff was not such a purist that he did not point out to his Board that this novelty might well animate the bank's trust business. He had a practical eye for the kind of individuals with large estates who would be attracted to protection against the future obliteration of the usefulness of their philanthropy and the memory of their names.

He was not discouraged by the skepticism of other bankers, a trace of which is found seven years after the Foundation was started, at the annual fun-poking dinner of Nisi Prius, the business lawyers' "playground" fraternity. One of its wags offered this parody, to the old hymn tune:

"How firm a Foundation for profits ahead
    Is laid for his bank by our excellent Fred.

What more could he do than to put this across?
A big stake to gain and no chance for a loss.

"What though Nutt and Sherwin their banks may combine,
Says Goff, 'I should worry, I've got my own line.
They bank for the living, I'll bank for the dead;
No runs on my bank, they can't draw out a red.' "

Mr. Goff listened to the song with every appearance of accepting its fun; but he must have felt some sense of an oblique indifference by others to something he had fashioned which even by that time had begun to make Cleveland a better and more enlightened city. The verse was lacking which might have acknowledged what the Foundation already had done to benefit public schools, recreation, and courts of Cleveland. However, humor is often unrelated to fact or justice.

News of the new Foundation spread promptly over the country, by press services, visiting reporters, and an energetic campaign from Mr. Goff's office to put its details before interested American leadership. Within ten days after the board's action, Andrew Carnegie, the best known philanthropist in the world, wrote that the plan "seemed well calculated to promote the important ends in view" and Robert S. Woodward, president of the Carnegie Institute, said: "It proves clearly that other people than Messrs. Carnegie and Rockefeller can do their parts equally with them toward the improvement of our race."

Starr J. Murphy, John D. Rockefeller's "secretary of philanthropy"; Frank A. Seiberling, president of Goodyear Tire & Rubber Co.; and William Nelson Cromwell, eminent New York lawyer, sent their endorsements. The aged Virgil P. Kline, the senior of Mr. Goff's old law firm, wrote: "I think the plan meets a want, and will be received with favor by donors and testators." The political firebrand Peter Witt said to Goff: "What a pity it was not thought of a long time ago! . . . Had it been, the people of this community would not only now be in possession of a fund to do many things the city cannot do, but many a beneficiary of unearned wealth would have been saved from an unhappy ending."

A surprised and thankful chorus went up from the directors and sponsors of the city's charity and welfare agencies. To that relatively small class then of responsible private citizens who supported and led these organizations the new Foundation must have risen like a sunburst.

CHAPTER II

The Foundation Stirs Up a City

THE INK WAS NOT DRY on the resolutions creating the Cleveland Foundation before Mr. Goff had moved in two directions to make the new agency an active thing. He determined on the most striking promotional program he could envision to make Cleveland aware of it, a series of community-wide public surveys through which the city would learn something about its principal problems. Then, with no funds in sight of the Foundation's own, he proposed to the bank directors that he personally and the bank share the expense of the program. Whether the joint contribution was equal has never been made known, but that Goff's share of this expense ran to many thousands of dollars was no secret.

Over the country, this was the era of celebrated and sometimes sensational investigation, starting with the magazine and newspaper muckrakers (President Theodore Roosevelt's term) and continuing through many congressional, legislative, aldermanic and private agency searchings for facts as to many facets of American political, sociological, and industrial life. It was the day of the Pujo committee, Gifford Pinchot, the elder Lafollette, Hiram Johnson. A leader like Fred Goff

would have flinched at the radical political objectives
and the slanted methods of some of these expeditions
into public sensation, but he argued to the bank directors
and others that the surest way to improvement of public
performances and remedy of social ills was to present
to the citizen opinion of any affected area all the exact,
uncolored fact of a matter warranting investigation and
let citizen opinion crystallize and apply the needed
changes.

In lieu of the Foundation's designated Distribution
Committee, and until there was Foundation income to
distribute, President Goff suggested a Foundation Survey Committee to be appointed by the formula adopted
by the bank — three members by the public officials,
two by the bank board. The directors appointed Charles
E. Adams, manufacturer and one of themselves, and
Bascom Little, head of a construction firm; Mayor
Newton D. Baker named Thomas G. Fitzsimons, a businessman friend of the Tom L. Johnson-Baker municipal
regime; the judges chose Miss Myrta L. Jones, a socially
aware member of an old Cleveland family, and Victor
W. Sincere, department store manager.

For survey director, Mr. Goff reached to Pittsburgh
for a welfare work leader already engaged in the kind
of social sifting Goff wanted. He was Allen T. Burns,
who had gone to Pittsburgh from social settlement and
Americanization work in Chicago at the Commons. His
activity there had led him to help found the School of
Social Work at the University of Chicago. Following
the investigation by a magazine (the forerunner of the

Survey Graphic) of the lot of the industrial workers in Pittsburgh, a Pittsburgh civic committee had been formed to try for a program of social welfare improvement, and Burns was its director for five years. He had become a local figure of importance and acquaintance. The committee's plans had taken shape with some effectiveness and acceptance.

The new committee and its survey director agreed on the first Foundation survey by mid-1914. That was a bad, hungry year for most American manufacturing centers, including Cleveland; the unemployed mounted ✓ to uncounted thousands and soup kitchens operated in the downtown streets. The short-comings of this human relief scared the inhabitants, and the Cleveland City Council in June asked the new Foundation framework to investigate public and private relief agencies looking to "any possible increase in efficiency, means of economy, methods of greater service, and plans for correlating the various resources and agencies."

By late summer, both the Associated Charities and the municipal relief department were on the verge of running out of funds.

Mr. Burns and the Survey Committee brought to Cleveland Sherman C. Kingsley, director of the Elizabeth McCormick Memorial Fund of Chicago, and Miss Amelia Sears, welfare director of the Cook County (Chicago) government. They began at once a study of municipal "outdoor relief," Associated Charities, Hebrew Relief Association, Salvation Army, juvenile court mother's pension, and public schools pension-relief operation. Their report was made and published on December 1.

The surveyors commended the Charities administration and demanded for it greatly increased financial support and improvement of staff by raising social training standards. They criticized the public relief for inadequacy, lack of comprehension of the relief problem, and no sense of responsibility. (They had discovered that the public relief director himself spent much of his time trying 3,708 pairs of shoes on indigents). Ten recommendations for changes in administration and operation were registered.

Almost every word of these reports was carried by the newspapers to the citizens, and Mr. Goff's theory of the results of enlightening the public began to pay out. It took a decade, and a public wrangle with one mayor who would have liquidated the public relief, to get the municipal operation modernized to the approximate limit of its resources; but within three years the Associated Charities found itself with four times its 1914 budget and a steady increase in professionally educated staff. Western Reserve University's School of Social Work got a springboard from this report. As a by-product, Mr. Kingsley came to Cleveland to become the first director of the new Cleveland Welfare Federation of social agencies — a vital step toward organization in 1918 of the Community Chest, the first in the United States.

Most of the virtues of this first survey drifted into history in the 1930's when public relief came to be a responsibility of national and state government, but in the first abyss of the great depression private relief agencies were using the 1914 findings as a first real analysis of problem, function, and responsibility.

This first survey had just aroused public consciousness when the new Cleveland Foundation enjoyed a windfall of national attention utterly unexpected. In 1914, the strike attempt at the Colorado Fuel & Iron Co., Rockefeller property, produced a class combat whose overtones stirred the country; and President Woodrow Wilson named a committee of which Frank P. Walsh, liberal labor lawyer, was chairman to probe the strike's actions and reactions. Walsh immediately pounced on the use of the great private Rockefeller Foundation to create and disseminate (Walsh charged) pro-enterprise and anti-labor sentiment. Late in 1914, Mr. Goff learned that the Walsh committee intended to investigate all foundations supported by wealth. The word "foundation" was coming into print to the man in the street with mysterious, awesome connotation, and Mr. Walsh was making the most of it.

The committee summoned the Rockefellers and their foundation board and staff for weeks of testimony, with whooping headlines; and when it finally finished with the last of these, John D. Rockefeller, Jr., it subpoenaed the massive J. P. Morgan the elder, and Fred H. Goff, president of Cleveland Trust and originator of a new foundation in Cleveland.

Mr. Goff took the stand. Mr. Walsh demanded how the Cleveland Foundation, created and supported by a trust company, went about infiltrating "conservative" opinion in its community. Mr. Goff surprised him at once by replying that the only public opinion the Cleveland Foundation could possibly generate would be by fact-finding investigations such as the Walsh committee itself was conducting.

Ah, said Walsh, but did not the bank influence the Foundation's viewpoints and selections of issues for investigation?

Mr. Goff cheerfully responded that the bank could not control the Foundation's actions — in fact, had chosen to abstain from control by placing everything in the hands of a term committee of citizens whose majority was appointed by public officials.

But this committee could in effect become self-perpetuating?

Certainly not, said Goff; the prevention of self-perpetuation was the hallmark and the key of this new kind of community trust. "Moreover," said the witness, "our trust, lacking the resources of Rockefellers, is especially open to poor people with enough idealism about small amounts of philanthropy to want these to be kept always useful as the years go by."

Walsh asked what were the resources of the Foundation. "We have no actual funds yet," said Goff, but added proudly, "we do have $40,000 already earmarked in wills, which is in sight upon the deaths of the donors."

Like an agile prosecutor, Walsh jumped to Goff's antipathy to self-perpetuating foundations and Mr. Goff was ready to agree that the probability of continuous close control was consideration for criticism of the Rockefeller and other private foundations. He reiterated this was the progressive novelty of the new Cleveland institution. Walsh complimented him roundly, and Goff left the stand to find that his testimony was the overwhelming feature of that and next day's copious newspaper accounts.

These newspaper and magazine reports and subsequent editorials about the new public trust in Cleveland launched Mr. Goff shortly on a popular newspaper and periodical advertising campaign — using magazine full pages and newspaper half pages — telling people what the Cleveland Foundation was, how it was democratically available, what community good it might do, how it protected philanthropic funds against the "dead hand." This advertising was fairly continuously maintained for nearly ten years and remains one of the most unusual pieces of financial advertising in the country's annals.

In 1916 Mr. Goff and Director Burns brought to Cleveland for survey purpose an individual destined to become one of the Foundation's finest minds and planners, as well as a brilliant analytical officer and economist (a term not born in 1916) for the Cleveland Trust Company. He was then Dr. Leonard P. Ayres, director of education research for New York's Russell Sage Foundation, and his immediate value was to organize a Foundation survey of Cleveland's disappointing, controversial public school system.

He became one of America's most outstanding statis-

ticians and interpreter of every kind of statistic. After
the first World War, he was "Col. Ayres" and after the
second "Gen. Ayres" for services in the United States
army which are singular to this day, for in both wars
he was the War Department's prime statistical officer.
Not merely of the logistics, expenditures, and man power
of war; in 1944, his report and analysis were the first
ever made of the location of wounds on fighting forces,
from which it was discovered that a terrible proportion
of these injuries were of the legs, thighs, and lower
abdomens from land mines and "booby traps," and
significantly changed battle tactics, reconnaissance, and
surgery. He had the interest of a Leonardo in everything he saw and studied, and the Foundation schools
investigation is one of two surveys whose results moved
a big city's operations to a permanently higher plane.

Cleveland schools had simmered with popular distrust for several years. Many felt the schools spent
too much for the level of educational results. School
board and superintendent fought each other. The
appearances of petty politics were numerous. Mr. Goff
wanted, for the Foundation's second public thrust, an
issue which would come close to hitting everyone's
interest, and nothing was more sadly "in the news"
than the schools.

Dr. Ayres observed early that it was probable that
the citizens did not actually know much about school
operations and laid out ten studies aimed to acquaint
people with the facts as to what day by day went on
in classrooms, board room, and school business offices.

Ayres picked a small staff who actually did little more than expose the facts. The reports were issued by the survey committee as fast as they were turned in. They were published seriatim in the papers, 25 in all by the beginning of 1917.

Based on the exposed facts, the probers made a number of recommendations which were at once adopted by public opinion and therefore by the school authorities. These took school board elections out of city politics and off by themselves; led to formation of an independent citizens committee to draft non-political leaders for the board and get them chosen; raised teacher salaries and training requirements (again, Western Reserve University found a stimulus for its School of Education); and established a tripartite schools administration composed of education, plant property, and finance. Ten years later, more than 90 of the 100 recommendations had been implemented, including the enlistment of Dr. Frank E. Spaulding from Columbia University Teachers College to be the superintendent to carry out the new order.

For more than thirty years, Cleveland's school system has never again sagged to the level which provoked the 1916 study, and has been held up many times as a model of organization and education standards. That the whole country became aware of the survey and its results is attested by the sale, in six years, of nearly 100,000 copies of findings, conclusions, and results. Mr. Goff had demonstrated again that to give the population the exact facts would lead to public remedy.

The Survey Committee decided late in 1916 on a survey of Cleveland's deficiencies in recreation, begun by Director Burns and Rowland Haynes, whom he brought from the east. American entry into World War I interrupted this study early, and late that year Mr. Burns decided to accept an invitation by the Carnegie Foundation to head an Americanization study, a field in which Burns had first and last been interested. In 1919 Professor Raymond Moley, then of the political science department of Western Reserve University, was asked to complete, with Haynes, the recreation investigation, which led to Moley's appointment as first full time Foundation director. Cleveland gained permanent benefits again from this survey. Its findings were separated into "Delinquency and Spare Time," "School Work and Spare Time," and "Wholesome Citizens and Spare Time," which contained 160 case histories from juvenile court, 100 of male and female "wholesome citizens," and samplings from the schoolrooms. Four reports were issued concerned with playgrounds, parks, libraries, settlements, the "Y" organizations, and commercial entertainment. Their effects were to found a municipal recreation department at the city hall, a Recreation Council under Welfare Federation sponsorship, a systematic summer playground program by city and schools administrations, a separate tax support for libraries, neighborhood centers in schools and city bath houses during evening hours, and city-guided sports leagues, both amateur and semi-professional. One of the best results was the birth of Cleveland's noted

Metropolitan Parks "emerald necklace," wooded and rural, which now stretches into five counties. The spark for it was a Recreation Council excursion by 50 leading Clevelanders to Bear Mountain (N. Y.) Park's "organized outdoors."

Mr. Haynes was induced to become the first director of the Recreation Council and served the community there through most of the 1920's.

A note on Director Burns' eventual career underlines the character of those in the Foundation's early years. Several years after the Carnegie Foundation survey, he became an outstanding authority, planner, and spokesman for the fast-growing Community Funds and United Appeals of the nation. He was one of the organizers of the Cleveland Community Chest, pioneer of the field, and retired a national figure.

Mr. Goff's program for the Foundation, suspended by the war in 1917, was by no means dormant; that same year, enough trusts had been made and testator promises received so that he could report that the Foundation would begin getting income of its own within a short time (actually, it was in 1919 that the first trust income came) and that the Cleveland Trust board had better animate its first Distribution Committee. The bank named Samuel Mather, distinguished capitalist and philanthropist, and Ambrose Swasey, industrialist — both bank directors — as its nominees. After long reflection, Mr. Mather declined the post and J. D. Williamson, banker and property owner, was selected. Mr. Swasey accepted appointment for a year and was succeeded by W. H. Prescott, banker and businessman.

The senior federal judge named Malcolm McBride, head of a wholesaling firm; the probate judge, Mr. Fitzsimons of the original survey committee; Mayor Harry L. Davis appointed Miss Belle Sherwin, civic and suffrage leader. Mr. Williamson was elected the first committee chairman.

Raymond Moley came to the directorship on invitation from the committee in 1919 from a teaching career shortly after winning a Ph.D. from Columbia University in the political science field. The first survey he conducted had its origins in the notorious subversive riot in Cleveland on May 1, 1919, in which pro-Soviet paraders provoked a bloody fight on the Public Square in which three were killed, and in the bombing of the home of Mayor Davis which was attributed by police to similar anti-American agents. The Foundation determined to investigate background and influences of the city's large foreign-born population, which was done chiefly by Dr. Joseph Remenyi, a sociological-literary figure of Hungarian origin who later became a popular professor of literature at Western Reserve. The survey recommended greater explanation of and militancy for American freedoms and folkways to the newer citizens, at schools and neighborhood centers.

In 1921, Moley directed a study of teacher training expansion in Cleveland's universities and colleges. But the most significant of the Moley surveys, and that which undoubtedly brought Cleveland the greatest reforms of this century, was the Cleveland Foundation inquiry in 1921-22 into the local administration of criminal justice. From it, the Cleveland Foundation derived attention from around the world.

Like most American industrial cities following World War I and the onset of the prohibition laws, Cleveland was experiencing an unparalleled increase in felonious crimes. These "waves," the newspapers headlined them, included daylight robbery-murders, killings of police, and a scandal involving a murder which touched the hem of the robe of the chief municipal judge. After a cold-blooded daytime murder of two well known industrialists for the Saturday payroll they were carrying, the Cleveland Automobile Club spent $25,000 on pursuit, conviction, and punishment of the killers.

A special grand jury impaneled by the state government at request of the Cleveland Bar Association broke down because witnesses defied the jury and escaped punishment from the jury's uncertain frame of mind. The Bar Association and the newspapers began to find ridiculous lapses of process in city and county criminal courts. Certain lawyers were identified as having grossly corrupt influence over courts and judges. Court records were discovered to have been stolen or tainted. A professor of sociology asked Director Moley what the Foundation might do about this frightening, unholy condition at about the time Fred Goff's lawyer-and-citizen instincts prodded him to speculations as to what had become of the old-time Cleveland sanctity of the courts of law. Moley volunteered to interest two of

Harvard Law School's most eminent teachers, Dean Roscoe Pound and Professor Felix Frankfurter, in an examination of the Cleveland breakdown, and Goff sent word to the mayor that a formal request on the Foundation to turn up the objective facts would be welcomed. The mayor and the Bar Association immediately filed a request for a survey of criminal justice and treatment of offenders, "such study to be the basis of constructive measures to improve the machinery for the administration of the law."

The Distribution Committee authorized the survey Jan. 4, 1921, after the Chamber of Commerce, Welfare Federation, League of Women Voters, and Federation of Women's Clubs had joined the appeal. Within a fortnight, Dean Pound and Professor Frankfurter accepted joint directorships and began to recruit an investigatory staff which included Reginald Heber Smith, Raymond Fosdick, Alfred Bettman, Dr. Herman Adler, Burdette G. Lewis, Herbert H. Ehrman, and Albert M. Kales. More than a dozen of the ablest Cleveland lawyers volunteered their services. Possibly no city in America ever has had the combined socio-legal talent of this group concentrated on finding what must be done for a grave lapse in society's protections.

Divided by Professor Frankfurter into task forces, the probers visited, interviewed, studied all records of, and even photographed all criminal courts and their staffs, the detention departments including police and sheriff, and the prosecuting agencies. The investigators found many evidences of wrong, evaded, and corrupt practices almost everywhere they looked, but regarded these as symptoms; they went on to find what the system needed to prevent or reduce these.

Each separate report was submitted to the public officials concerned and findings of fact verified or agreed on as nearly as possible. Then each of more than twenty reports was made public as broadly as possible. Besides the hundreds of columns in the newspapers, they were delineated in 67 speeches at public assemblies in Cleveland and 25 outside the city. Director Moley conducted a seminar on the findings before a women's club in ten sessions with an average attendance of 500.

Some of the courts' troubles ended with mere publication; some few minor public placeholders quietly disappeared or retired. The community almost trenchantly accepted every survey recommendation, with a sense of relief and revived purpose.

As proposed by the survey, fourteen Cleveland citizen organizations joined to create the Association for Criminal Justice, to be watchman of the court reforms. With paid director and staff, the association endured into the 1950's, when its service appeared no longer necessary.

The courts set up a card index of crimes and criminals which does still operate. New liaison relations were founded between city and county criminal courts and prosecutors. Trial courts installed psychiatry and compulsory probation staff recommendations for every case. As an offshoot, the Bar Association undertook to take judicial election campaigns out of politics; after forty years, its election influence has become as great as or even greater than the partisan political organizations in judicial contests. All offices concerned with the courts were mandated to improve records, procedure, and staff training.

Records of two current years are eloquent testimony to the survey's objectives and achievement. Per annum, from 1920 through 1922, Greater Cleveland had 489 fewer robberies, 947 fewer automobiles stolen, and 901 fewer burglaries.

For the next twenty years, the account of the Cleveland Foundation's cause, action, and results in its survey of criminal justice went over the world. Some law schools installed it as "case reading." The London Times published book reviews of the volumes of the survey reports, as did American law journals. The "Survey Graphic" devoted an entire issue to the study and its results. A former Lord Chancellor of England wrote to Mr. Moley: "These are books which will be studied exhaustively in many countries." For ten years, letters of inquiry about the survey came to the Foundation from three continents.

The job on the courts made nearly every adult in Cleveland acquainted with the Foundation. A faith began to bud that the Foundation might survey any city troubles and produce a reform. Out of a squabble over the wisdom and the acoustics of the city's big new Public Hall about to be finished the Foundation had a City Council resolution begging it to survey the situation, usefulness, and future of the new auditorium. A brand new mayor declared it a "white elephant" and said he would never open it unless he could be shown it would run itself.

Mr. Goff disdained a survey of such a matter as too political and parochial, but it was characteristic of him (and the respect in which he was held) that he settled the Public Hall "crisis" in less than an hour and 500 spoken words one afternoon. He was one of fifty business-men to accept the mayor's invitation to a meeting on the matter; after the mayor had outlined his laissez faire position and a few visitors had hemmed and hawed, Goff said he believed the mayor completely right that the auditorium should have to support itself, and proposed that a businessmen's committee take over its future and control. This was adopted with such unanimity Mr. Goff was able to lead the meeting across the street so it could informally test the hall's suspect acoustics.

This independent management got the Cleveland Public Hall off to a long and useful career, and it rarely was mentioned again as a municipal issue.

Disposition of the new Distribution Committee, now that the Foundation was receiving income, to argue the cost of city-wide surveys of public matters as against benefactions more clearly philanthropic, was evident by 1923 in the last year of Mr. Goff's life. He believed the surveys had put the Foundation into local consciousness as nothing else would have done, and he was sensitive enough to local public administrations to believe the Foundation could become their permanent watchdog; but he was unable to contest the final authority of the

Distribution Committee's choice of policy, and must also have realized that his program for arresting popular attention — at no inexpensive price — had about matured. Moley's predilection for public affairs made him agree with Goff that the public investigations were the Foundation's broadest possible services; he resigned in 1923 to accept a Columbia University chair of government when it became clear that future surveys supported by the Foundation would be delegated to other agencies.

Raymond Moley is another of the striking figures developed in the Foundation's first decade. At Columbia, he became the confidant, adviser, and speech writer for Gov. Franklin D. Roosevelt, then Assistant Secretary of State in President Roosevelt's first term; departing from Roosevelt because of the president's subsequent turn toward economic and political absolutism, he made himself nationally known as author of political histories, editor, and today the most veteran commentator in print on national affairs.

Yet the ten years of community surveys and their helpful results stand almost alone in the history of the good accomplished across this country by community trusts. It is hardly too much, in hindsight, to judge that they rescued the city of Cleveland on several frontiers. Looking back after forty years, Dr. Moley says of them: "The pattern of the Foundation's concerns served as an agency which endeavored to concentrate on city-wide problems, consider them from a measurably detached position, and create a climate of opinion in which improvements could be made. Whether with larger funds it would have been prudent to continue the surveys, I hesitate to venture opinion. I was in an excellent position to realize such surveys arouse controversy; old habits and old forms of institutional life had of necessity to be criticized. But in general the Foundation had public opinion on its side.

"There were problems, when I left, appropriate for Foundation research. The development of Cleveland's lake front, needing planning and large government and philanthropic money; a need for planned smoke abatement; an overhaul of property assessment to create a more orderly and beautiful metropolitan area. In some of these, other institutions made contributions. I do venture to claim the Foundation's explorations did a great deal to awaken the city to the need for self-appraisal, however painful."

Mr. Goff died after a brief illness March 14, 1923. A whole city's sense of shock and loss could be felt. The memorial resolution by the Foundation Distribution Committee said of him: "Founder and unfailing source of inspiration, guidance, and support, nine years ago Mr. Goff brought into existence the Cleveland Foundation as a community trust dedicated to the task of carrying forward civic progress and human welfare . . . a new form of benefaction carefully designed by its founder to be flexible in plan, democratic in spirit and method, deriving its powers from the people, and to the last analysis responsible to the public for its acts.

". . . The founder has passed, but his work goes on; and to the carrying forward of the plans and hopes that he conceived we, the members of the Cleveland Foundation Committee, pledge our every effort and our unremitting zeal."

The multiple trusteeship never had left Mr. Goff's mind. He believed no other progress would so register community faith in the Foundation and its aims and that it would bring in funds of civic-interested persons whose trusts were in the other banks and provide the other banks with an appeal which the Cleveland Trust Company was finding valuable. Fred W. Ramsey, a director, urged steps to align other banks in the Foundation a year after Mr. Goff's death, and the Distribution Committee the same year named a sub-committee to discuss multiple trusteeship with the Cleveland Trust board. In 1927, Warren S. Hayden, private banker and alert citizen, urged drafting of a multiple trusteeship form of resolution on President Harris Creech, Mr. Goff's successor at Cleveland Trust, and President Creech appointed Mr. Freiberger, head of the trust department, Mr. Sawyer, counsel, and Col. Ayres, by then a vice president with principal assignment to Foundation affairs.

The draft was produced after a year of discussion; a directors' committee studied revisions of it, then employed John E. Morley and James R. Garfield as special counsel on the final draft. President Creech then notified heads of the four other major banks of this move and invited in their counsel and officers.

The original skepticism in the other banks about the Foundation's character and usefulness had long since disappeared. President Wilbur Baldwin of the Union Trust Co., then the largest institution; President J. Arthur House of the Guardian Trust Co., President Corliss E. Sullivan of Central United Bank, and President John Sherwin, Jr., of the Midland Bank, at once accepted the invitation, and agreement was reached December 5, 1930, on a uniform resolution for each bank. Between December 23 and January 13, 1931, boards of all five banks enacted the multiple trusteeship resolution.

A few guide-lines were modified by the multiple trusteeship. In place of the one bank board, a committee of five bank presidents became the trustee authority and nominator of two of the Distribution Committee. Scope of the Foundation was widened to the state of Ohio, and bequests which failed to name a trustee would be assigned by the Trustees Committee to one of the trustee banks. The new resolution was built on the framework of the original 1914 resolution including such provisions as that no more than two of the Distribution Committee could be of the same religious sect, nor could any public office holder be appointed.

For disbursements of principal, each trustee bank was given final say by two-thirds vote of its directors. In case of transfer of a worn-out or impractical philanthropic provision, consent must be by four of the Distribution Committee and two-thirds of the directors of the trustee bank. Any tie vote in the Trustees Committee would be settled by majority vote of the committee and the Distribution Committee.

The multiple trusteeship was announced at a civic dinner January 6, 1931, when the origin of the Foundation was narrated by former Secretary of War Baker; Mr. Goff's hope for this progress told by Mr. Hayden; and the advantages of the multiple trusteeship set forth by Ralph Hayes, director of the New York Community Trust. Mr. Baker's prime figure of speech, a form for which he was oratorically famous, was that the new step was "an appropriate development of the original idea that once was so new and so unusual that perhaps it had to be kept under the glass case of the inventor to protect it from ill and unaccustomed winds, but now had become so sturdy that it could be another element in this cemented process of Cleveland as a self-conscious community."

Appropriate also was Ralph Hayes' appearance. From 1920 to 1923 he had been Mr. Goff's assistant at Cleveland Trust and was imbued and indoctrinated about the Foundation. In his last year, Mr. Goff had suggested he go lend a hand to the budding New York Community Trust; Mr. Hayes went and became that foundation's first and only director. "Mr. Goff's concern," he reported many years later, "seemed to be that the New York fund's concept should not be so absorbed or influenced by any one group as to impair its dedication to the public." This was not Fred Goff's least contribution to the community trusts of America.

CHAPTER III

The Spread Across the Country

THE IDEA of the community foundation to work to defeat the "dead hand" and to bring into existence new forces for concentrated community welfare spread across the country almost immediately on Cleveland's beginning in 1914. Mr. Goff, the creator, helped considerably. He recommended and advertised the Cleveland plan to the bank and lawyer friends he had over the country; he went to a number of interested cities to explain and counsel them in their starts on community trusts; he was evangelistic inside the Trust Company Division of the American Bankers Association.

In 1915, nine community foundations were founded: the Chicago Community Trust, Detroit Community Trust, Milwaukee Foundation, Minneapolis Foundation, St. Louis Community Trust, Los Angeles Community Trust, Spokane Foundation, Attleboro (Mass.) Foundation, and the Committee of the Permanent Charity Fund of Boston. (The Los Angeles Trust became the California Community Foundation.)

There were five more in 1916: The Indianapolis Foundation, Cambridge (Mass.) Foundation, Honolulu Hawaiian Foundation, Providence Rhode Island Foundation, and Williamsport (Pa.) Foundation.

In 1918, the Philadelphia Foundation and the Youngstown (O.) Foundation began; in 1919, the Buffalo Foundation, Quincy (Ill.) Foundation, Richmond Foundation, Tulsa Permanent Community Trust, and Winston-Salem Foundation; in 1920, the Delaware Foundation at Wilmington, the Harrisburg Foundation, the Plainfield (N.J.) Foundation.

The first out-of-country foundation was begun at Winnipeg, Manitoba, in 1921, as were the Maine Charity Foundation of Portland and the Dayton Foundation. Grand Rapids and Ashtabula (O.) Foundations came in 1922; in 1923, the New York Community Trust, the Louisville Foundation, and the Scarsdale (N.Y.) Foundation. In 1924, the Altoona Foundation and the Lancaster County (Pa.) Foundation. In 1925, the Denver Foundation, Kalamazoo Foundation, and Hartford Foundation for Public Giving. In 1926, the Battle Creek Foundation and the Kenosha (Wis.) Foundation. So in the first twelve years, 40 present community trusts in 22 states, one territory, and one other country were set up in appreciation of the new kind of establishment for trusteed philanthropy.

An even higher count was given at the 1925 convention of trust departments of the American Bankers Association; the number of community trusts and agencies resembling them was put by a speaker at 55. This division of the bank association already had created a standing committee, with annual report, on community foundations.

J. Lionberger Davis, director of the St. Louis Union

Trust Co., around which the St. Louis Community Trust was founded, reported late in 1915 that nine foundations had been founded on the Cleveland design and that one of the key principles of all nine was "the Cleveland Foundation . . . protection of purpose by giving fullest publicity" to the new community trusts' operations and public aims. He included a glimpse of the Cleveland Foundation's estimates of its own prospects: "Mr. Goff reports upward of $30,000,000 has been pledged to the Cleveland Foundation under deeds of trust and by wills within a year after the announcement of the plan; though in most cases the donors have reserved the use of the income during their lives, or directed payment of income to members of their families during their lives." Since this was the same year in which Goff had told the Walsh Committee at Washington that these prospects were $40,000, the chance of a misprint seems possible; the original Foundation had been in existence only a year.

The first two years of the foundation spread brought two significant expansions of the Cleveland design. In founding the Chicago Community Trust, the Harris Trust & Savings Co. was given a $200,000 fund by Albert W. Harris and others for general administrative expenses of the new community foundation; in 1916, the Indianapolis Foundation was the first to set off with a multiple trusteeship.

Another diversion from the Cleveland design appeared in the early years of the community foundation's spread. Because of state laws or local situation, foundations were incorporated instead of created by bank resolutions in the Minneapolis, Richmond, and Winnipeg establishments. So was the Distribution Committee of the Boston Permanent Charity Fund; after 1931, incorporation was made of the Kalamazoo Foundation Distribution Committee; Battle Creek, Santa Barbara, and Watertown (N.Y.) Foundations incorporated at their start.

By 1931, the Bankers Association Trust Company Division reported the existence of 74 community trusts, exactly half of them with multiple trusteeships. The division's standing committee had put into these words the purpose of the foundations: "The Community Trust is a recognition of two fundamental facts; (1) of the element of certain and constant change which is taking place in our social structure and in our viewpoint with respect to charities; and (2) that the charitable problems of each generation can better be solved by the best minds of these generations than through the medium of the dead hand of the past."

In her history of community foundations for the National Council on Community Foundations in 1961, Mrs. Wilmer Shields Rich, the council executive, traced three periods of growth: — The first fifteen years, before the "great depression," in which motivation came from bankers, creating community trusts in most of the larger American cities; a second fifteen years of lull, during which growth was negligible because of the depression's and the war years' effects on philanthropy; and a third period up to the present time in which the banker motivation was accompanied by that of citizens concerned with planning capital gifts for community use, a revival period which re-accelerated the development nation wide.

The lull of the middle period reduced nearly a score of established foundations to practical inactivity. Some of these revived and flourish today. This dull period was characterized also by suspension in 1933 of the Trust Company Division, A. B. A., standing committee on community trusts. It was in 1949 that new national leadership evolved with the organization of the National Committee on Foundations and Trusts for Community Welfare. It helped greatly to revitalize and to start up foundations over the land, the national joint and mutual interests growing in 1957 into the National Council, with staff offices.

Among the earliest and largest community trusts started in the year after the Cleveland Foundation began, it is not easy to trace where the idea was first discussed as among Chicago, Boston, or St. Louis. The published story of the Chicago Trust reports that Norman Wait Harris of Chicago's Harris Trust & Savings Bank met the president of the St. Louis Union Trust Co. in mid-1914 on a liner returning from Europe and heard from him of plans in St. Louis to found a community trust; and that Mr. Harris's son and colleague, Albert Wadsworth Harris, visited the St. Louis bank and got there a copy of the resolution and declaration of trust adopted by the Cleveland Trust Company to establish the Cleveland Foundation. In or perhaps before the same weeks and months, Charles E. Rogerson, president of the

Boston Safe Deposit & Trust Co., was discussing a community trust project with his lawyer son, Charles M. Rogerson.

At least, their histories can be described as concurrent. All three were set up with original single bank trusteeships, though the Committee of the Permanent Charity Fund of Boston was incorporated.

In Chicago, Albert W. Harris discussed the community foundation with scores of judges, lawyers, business leaders, investment counsel, educators, and philanthropists — one a future governor of Illinois, the then Probate Judge Henry A. Horner. On May 12, 1915, the Harris Trust & Savings board adopted the similar resolution and declaration of trust and the Cleveland proposal for term appointment of five members of a Distribution Committee, two by two judges, one by Chicago's mayor, two by the trust company. A former judge, a trust officer, a railroad president, a Harris Trust director, and a business lawyer were the first selections. At the committee's first meeting, Albert Harris offered to pay personally all expenses for one year for an executive director and an office. After his father's death in 1916, Albert and others established a general fund of $200,000 for the foundation's support and shortly afterwards a $400,000 special fund as a memorial to his father.

Late in 1916, Fred Goff was invited from Cleveland to tell 350 Chicago civic leaders about these foundation developments. One result was a much more lively interest on the part of other Chicago banks in the new instrument, and it was somewhat in the nature of following public opinion that, within two years, Harris and the committee organized an advisory committee of the chief executives of five other banks and six prominent business and professional men. This proved an effective way in which to interest and inform a great deal of the financial and industrial community of the new foundation's function and performance; in fact, it was not until the late 1940's under the leadership of Edward L. Ryerson that the Chicago Community Trust embraced its multiple trusteeship. A singular feature is that any bank or trust company in Cook County may be a trustee.

Within four years, and in spite of the practical shutdown on growth compelled by World War I, the Chicago Trust had capital funds of $725,000 and had distributed $67,520 income. Beginning in 1919, the foundation set about a series of factual surveys for the public weal along the lines which had swiftly acquainted Cleveland with its new foundation. That was a year of post-war hubbub over the character of the foreign-born population (and of some hasty emotional governmental acts and attitudes toward the foreign-born); the Community Trust employed Frank Denman Loomis, who became its secretary and executive for twenty-nine years, to conduct research and report on Chicago's Americanization services.

It was news to some, from this survey report, that 56 percent of the residents of Chicago had been reared in foreign languages. It found that a large number of agencies, from night schools to settlement houses and particular industries were coping inadequately with the Americanization task. A prompt and vigorous result of this first Community Trust survey was the formation of a Greater Chicago Americanization Council, which under the leadership of a widely respected banker, expanded and emphasized the education of the foreign-born over several years, after which the post-war problems seemed to have been dispelled.

Requests were immediate for a miscellany of other surveys by the Community Trust. Housing for a record influx of young women was investigated under direction of Elizabeth Trotter, with results of some expansion of suitable residence and creation of a central registry. A survey of prenatal care led by Mrs. Adena Miller Rich produced an enlargement of public and private infant welfare stations.

The most conspicuous survey was that requested by the Cook County commissioners of Chicago's squalid and unsafe old county jail, to examine which the Community Trust hired Dr. George W. Kirchwey, expert criminologist and law school dean of New York. After nearly a year's study and investigation, Dr. Kirchwey's reports urged a new and modern jail, renovation of the old for practical short-term purposes, and segregation of young offenders in reformatories or farm colonies. The recommendation attracted public, professional, and newspaper support far and wide, but political involvement eventually led to a new jail adjacent to the old in disregard of the survey. "Forty years later," Mr. Loomis reported in 1961, "there is mounting public demand that the Bridewell be modernized, its treatment of criminals be humanized, and a new jail and criminal courts building be built closer to the commercial and civic center of the city."

Under Community Trust auspices, there were surveys of the care of ex-veterans in Chicago, especially in the Veterans' Administration hospitals, and of the care of crippled children (for the supporting Chicago Rotary Clubs.) Both were directed by Mrs. Henry T. Paulson, social care authority. Perhaps it was partly from these surveys that the Chicago Community Trust received its first large gift in 1924 — $1,000,000 from James A. Patten, the income to be distributed to designated institutions.

The Chicago Community Trust was a leader in the enlivening and enlargement during the 1930's of Chicago's Community Fund, and its directors were encouraged toward warm and knowledgeable relations with the social and welfare councils of the city.

Boston's Committee of the Permanent Charity Fund was the first of the community trusts to be given a sizeable bequest in its early years, — two years in fact after its formation by the Boston Safe Deposit & Trust Co. James M. Longley, a director of the bank, became President Rogerson's most convinced advocate of the new idea and his bequest on his death in 1917 at once gave the fund $2,836,553, ultimately a total of $4,312,482. Three other bequests, one the largest ever assigned to an American community foundation, eventually raised the Boston fund to one of the three largest.

These were the Albert Stone, Jr., bequest (1959) of $19,414,771; $2,549,743 by his sister Mary Stone (1948); and $3,018,816 by Edith M. Ashley (1960).

The Boston fund is one of forty in this country which remain with a single trustee. Charles M. Rogerson, the lawyer son of the president, author of the trust agreement and declaration, served as secretary and treasurer on a part-time basis until his death in 1945; Arthur G. Rotch then was named as successor, and became director in 1959; the full-time director now is Wilbur J. Bender.

The St. Louis Union Trust Co. directors, at request of a citizens' committee, adopted a foundation resolution modeled on the Cleveland procedure on January 21, 1915. The community trust did not become active until 1948, when a substantial share of the F. William Weinheimer estate came to it for distribution; in 1949, the residue of the John L. Messmore estate was transmitted to the St. Louis Community Trust 35 years after Mr. Messmore's death. An appointed Distribution Committee, three chosen by two judges and the mayor, two by the bank trustee, has had a pattern of grants to the St. Louis United Fund (Community Chest).

The original multiple trusteeship for an American community trust was implemented in 1916 by the Indianapolis Foundation, at its start, at the judgment of Evans Woollen, president of the Fletcher Savings & Trust Co., one of the banker friends of Fred H. Goff — Mr. Woollen was the pioneer in Indiana of the foundation movement. When his trust company adopted the resolution to create the community trust on January 6,

1916, he at once invited two other banks with trust operations to join as trustees, the Indiana Trust Co. and the Union Trust Co. of Indianapolis, and they immediately accepted.

The descendants or successors to all three banks are trustees today, the American Fletcher National Bank & Trust Co., the Merchants National Bank & Trust Co., and the Indiana National Bank; in 1961, the Peoples Bank & Trust Co. became the fourth trustee. There is evidence that Mr. Woollen both appreciated and confirmed the diversion he introduced; in 1922, he commissioned one of the Foundation staff to visit the other large-city foundations to note their progress, and in this report several advantages of the multiple trusteeship are heavily underlined.

In the Indianapolis Foundation history is a story of lightning-like fortune not quite to be paralleled elsewhere. After its beginning, the community trust had slow going, like most of the new agencies. Late in 1921, without notice, it received a bequest of $300,000 from a philanthropist who had never actually lived in Indianapolis; six months later, a trust of almost a million dollars was handed to it; three months after that, a bequest of a million and a half came to the Foundation. In less than a year, the Indianapolis Foundation had shot up to one of the largest in the nation. Incidentally, the trusts came to the Foundation through different banks.

The $300,000 fund came from Alphonse P. Pettis, who was retired on the French Riviera, and many years before had built and sold a profitable dry goods store of the city. He told the merchant who was his successor of a longing to do something, after death, to fulfill an obligation he felt from having prospered in Indianapolis; the friend, when the Indianapolis Foundation was announced, sent him detailed accounts of it and a note, "Maybe this was what you were looking for." From Nice, France, Mr. Pettis sent word of his desire to have the new Foundation administer his funds.

The second fund was that of James E. Roberts, who was consulting his lawyer about rewriting his will to take advantage of the new community trust at the exact time Mr. Pettis was studying the Foundation on the sunny shore of the Mediterranean. The third fund was that of Delavan Smith, publisher of the Indianapolis News, a bachelor. All three funds were bestowed without restriction as to their application.

The Winston-Salem Foundation was created in 1919 under the guidance of Colonel F. H. Fries, then president of Wachovia Bank and Trust Company, who was a close personal friend of Mr. Goff. It is now by far the largest community trust in the South with assets of about $20,000,000 although no full time executive was appointed until 1961 when James A. Gray became Executive Director.

Personal acquaintance with Fred H. Goff and his foundation led to formation of two other well-known community trusts, Pittsburgh and Columbus. Aims C. Coney was a Cleveland banker who went to Pittsburgh and became head of the trust department of the Union

Trust Co. of Pittsburgh, later the Mellon National Bank & Trust Co. He began preaching the success of the Cleveland Foundation to Pittsburgh in the 1940's, and in 1945 the Pittsburgh Foundation was formed with the help of the instrument supporting the Cleveland Foundation and counseling from the Cleveland Foundation director, Leyton E. Carter. It is distinctive for its guardianship of outmoded charity funds from the county Orphans' Court and of assets of extinct charitable institutions and associations; one of these was composed of a refund from oversubscription in 1871 of the Pittsburgh philanthropy to victims of the Chicago fire! Its income has subsidized city planning — in a city in which planning has been live and famous — and a great deal of education, including music and art education. From the beginning, the Pittsburgh Foundation saw the wisdom of employing an able, full-time director, Stanton Belfour having served continuously in that post.

The Columbus Foundation resulted from Freda Goff having been a Vassar classmate and a bridesmaid for Mary White, whose husband Harrison Sayre came to know Mr. Goff thereby. Sayre and his friends nursed the Goff foundation idea for twenty years before it could be locally implemented through an unrestricted fund coming to the Alfred L. Willson Charitable Foundation; this was made the signal for a public appeal for a community trust. Two banks were originally trustees, and a third enlisted. A great identification of the Columbus Foundation came from its distribution of nearly a half million dollars to the city's hospital expansion program. Mr. Sayre subsequently became president of the National Council on Community Foundations.

The big New York Community Trust, to whose birth Goff dispatched Ralph Hayes in 1923 as expert from the Cleveland Foundation's eight years of growth, came about as much by crystallization of interest by several New York banks and trust companies as by anything else, and, as in Cleveland, a great idea was chartered without a penny of assets. The public appeal from the start was to direct philanthropic funds to eligible trustee banks for custody and investment, these to use the services of the joint trust's distribution committee. As with the pioneer foundation, the committee would give expression to founders' desires but effect such future adjustments as changing conditions might invite. As in Cleveland, composition of the committee provided a minority of appointments from the participant trustees, a majority from appointees by the mayor, the senior federal appellate judge, and the presidents of the Association of the Bar, Academy of Medicine, Chamber of Commerce, and Brooklyn Institute of Arts and Sciences.

The New York Community Trust originated a trustees' committee to assume the foundation responsibility exercised elsewhere individually by trustee banks.

In its first year, there was no rush of bequests to the New York trust, but in 1925 Mr. and Mrs. Felix M. Warburg committed a $500,000 Moritz & Charlotte Warburg memorial fund, and Mrs. Warburg a similar trust as memorial to her father Jacob H. Schiff.

Unusual recognition came to the New York trust in 1928 when that eminent philanthropist John D. Rockefeller, Jr. transferred to it from previous private trusteeship, $2,500,000 of the Laura Spelman Rockefeller Memorial. This helped to perpetuate the memory of Mr. Rockefeller's mother after dissolution of the original fund.

The Philadelphia Foundation had private origin in 1918 when the Fidelity-Philadelphia Trust Co. established, under that name, its private charitable arm. Except in public appointment system, the trust functioned conventionally. In 1958, a community group headed by Graeme Lorimer (now the chairman of the Foundation's Distribution Committee) proposed it be expanded into a community trust. Five other banks joined the Fidelity-Philadelphia Trust as trustees, and a distribution committee was set up by appointment of two trustee nominees and one each from the city's university presidents, Bar Association, Chamber of Commerce, and Welfare Council. The Foundation now has a full time executive, Sidney Repplier.

In the beginning, community foundations were established in the larger cities where there was a concentration of potential donors and affluence. In more recent years smaller communities have launched foundations, some with conspicuous success. One such is the Spartanburg County Foundation of South Carolina. Established in 1943 in a county with a population of only 130,000 it now has assets of nearly $2,000,000 and has disbursed more than $900,000 for charitable and educational purposes in the past 18 years. Two key persons in this success story have been Walter S. Montgomery, a textile mill president, and Benjamin O. Johnson, attorney. Both have also served as officers of the National Council on Community Foundations.

Some of the smaller city community trusts, as in earlier days, have used the survey to gain popular attention. The Norfolk (Va.) Foundation, established in 1950, conducted a study of education and opportunity in nursing for Negro girls which demanded considerable local interest.

An early foundation, that of Buffalo, opened in 1919, was fortunate in attracting several sizable bequests in its first few years, and, as does the Milwaukee Foundation (and the Philadelphia Foundation until 1958) serves to show how original single trusteeships may of themselves attract a significant amount of funds.

On the other hand, the multiple trusteeship became a pattern for most of the subsequent foundations after the New York Community Trust's example of six bank trustees which over the years became twelve. This was because financial institutions and other agencies look to New York as the loftiest fiscal capital. If, in the nation's largest and richest center, a combination of bank trust departments was the modus vivendi, then that was to most people the accepted way.

A long-term deliberateness in getting a community trust under full sail is a characteristic of perhaps a dozen of today's foundations, in whose communities the ideal and operation were discussed, endorsed, and promoted for a long period before actual founding. The San Francisco Community Foundation was projected in 1926 by a citizen group whose total personal capital was impressive; meetings and publicity drew in some of the best-known family names in the city. It was not until 1948, when a private charitable foundation invigorated the community trust purpose, that the San Francisco Foundation was stimulated into existence, depression and the years of World War II having had a negative reaction on the primary enthusiasm. An interesting circumstance is that the family names of the early projectors, such as Crocker, Koshland, and Roth, appear, in the second generation, in today's distribution committee of the Foundation. Among the foundation's funds are Crocker, Alexander, Fleishhacker, Haas, Merrill, and Stern trust funds from similar names of those absorbed with the 1926 development. The San Francisco Foundation has all nine of the city's trust companies as trustees, — so that it is figuratively the case that the community trust did have a start of a sort back in the 1920's.

The vigorous development of the San Francisco Foundation in a relatively short period of time provides another example of the value of competent full-time direction. John R. May was appointed executive director in 1948 when the Foundation office was first opened.

An act by the provincial legislature of Manitoba was employed to create the Winnipeg Foundation in 1921, first outside the United States. This act gave to the trust companies title control, custody, and management of assets and to the foundation trustees, called an "advisory board," transfers, assignments, and conveyances of the properties, with co-execution by the bank trustee. The Winnipeg Foundation began its existence with a $100,000 bequest of W. F. Alloway, a banker, whose subsequent gifts to philanthropy through the foundation amounted (with his wife's) to $1,500,000.

Alloway is one of the romantic figures in the narratives of North America's foundations, for as a youth born in Montreal he first saw the trading town of Winnipeg as a soldier in Col. Sir Garnett Wolseley's Red River military expedition against the western Indians. Young Alloway liked the looks of Winnipeg and settled there to make his fortune; his material success made him forever conscious of a gratitude to the community as he watched and helped it grow into a Canadian metropolis.

Among many other beneficiaries, the University of Manitoba owes to the Winnipeg Foundation its School of Social Work. Peter B. Lowe, who helped to organize the Foundation and served as its executive director for 27 years, retired in 1957 and was succeeded by Hugh A. Benham.

The first detailed country-wide report on the progress of the community trusts was made in 1950 by the National Committee on Foundations and Trusts for Community Welfare, forerunner of the present National Council on Community Foundations, Inc. The National Committee was organized in 1949 with Edward L. Ryerson of Chicago as its first chairman, to furnish a medium for the exchange of information and aid the development of community trusts. The 1950 report was authored by Frank D. Loomis of the Chicago Community Trust assisted by an advisory committee of such foundation pioneers as Stanton Belfour of Pittsburgh, James Brown IV of Chicago, Leyton Carter of Cleveland, John May of San Francisco, Harrison Sayre of Columbus, and Ralph Blanchard who was then Executive Director of Community Chests and Councils of America. The report listed 115 foundations of community public character as having been launched since the Cleveland Foundation's birth; of which 25 could not be traced, having either been dissolved or become inactive.

"Glowing expectancy of large and easy money," reported Loomis, "which seems to have animated many early Community Trusts has seldom been realized. Three or four early trusts were fortunate in having substantial funds turned over to them for administration soon after they were organized. Most of the community trusts which have achieved any success at all soon found they would have to settle down to hard work, to diligent, patient, intelligent promotion of the community trust idea on its merits. That such efforts have been rewarded is another evidence of the soundness of the idea."

Some few distribution committees, Mr. Loomis added, seemed to have become dormant or "relegated to the inept position of being merely advisory to the bank trustee which has assumed full control of the entire enterprise." Others, he said, complained they had no real discretion as to disbursement or policy "since nearly all gifts are strictly for designated institutions and their approval of appropriations is perfunctory."

It seems reasonable to assume that the late mid-years of the community trust development would produce some mortality and some instances of less than purposeful functioning. But the acceleration in growth of foundation assets and diversions of distribution since 1950 changed and remedied whatever tendencies these suggested.

CHAPTER IV

Profile of the Pioneer
Community Foundation

I N 1923, the year of Fred H. Goff's death, the Cleveland Foundation had grown to capital assets of $367,452 (ledger value) — and had income for distribution of $7,637.

Nothing tells its narrative of progress better than inspection of these sums each decade since. In 1933, assets had reached $5,916,689, and a distribution of $175,519. In 1943, the assets were $8,362,162, and the year's distribution of $213,523 was having impact on all Cleveland. But the great growth was ahead.

The 1953 statistics were: Assets $17,702,301, and the annual distribution that year went over a half million at $543,500. The preliminary report for 1962—one year short of a fifth decade—listed capital of $46,091,203 in 118 separate funds having a market value of nearly $75,000,000 and $2,260,766 paid out in grants. Among community foundations it was first in America in amount of grants distributed from income (as contrasted with grants from principal); and first in total and in active capital.

The cold statistics of a half century of philanthropy kept fresh and current disclose an amazing variety of usefulness. In its lifetime total of $18,000,000 in grants, the Cleveland Foundation has given funds to 22 colleges, four secondary schools, 30 hospitals, 18 medical and health agencies, ten educational bureaus or ventures, hundreds of students, 50 civic, cultural, art, music, or drama operations, more than 60 operating agencies of social welfare, more than 70 local and national administrative social organizations; and has among these financed more than 30 surveys and special research studies in health, geriatrics, community planning at several levels, alcoholism, medicine, nursing, education at several age plateaus, unemployment and rehabilitation, recreation of many sorts, community centers, social work administration, public charity, child care, population growth, conservation of natural resources, theater, restoration of neighborhoods, the public courts, police problems, teaching upgrading, assimilation, hospital administration, specific diseases, health hazards, nutrition, and psychiatry. After 1924 the Foundation left the direct survey field and made grants to other agencies to carry on this kind of work.

These statistics show that in numbers of grants the Foundation has devoted its attention largely to social welfare, next to education, next to health. Yet within these hundreds of grants are some fascinating purposes connected with water supply, music as psychiatric therapy, the encouragement of private gardens and horticulture, a camp for diabetic children, a civic club's public forum, a Great Lakes Exposition on Cleveland's lake front, three kinds of symphony orchestras (including the notable Cleveland Orchestra), a Negro theater, the revival out of a slum, specialized city planning, the reform of adolescent speech and arithmetic, choral singing, a town meetings program, a prized woodland arboretum, a successful traffic safety campaign, and an electronic aid for a university library.

The Foundation has provided the impetus for the launching of many pioneering services and new agencies in Greater Cleveland. Among these "firsts" are T. B. detection programs in hospitals, the Law-Medicine Center and the Center on Mental Development at Western Reserve University, Cleveland Commission on Higher Education, Educational Research Council, Center on Alcoholism, Golden Age Center, Poison Information Center, Legal Aid Public Defender, Foster Home Recruiting Service and the International Youth Leaders Exchange Program.

Many of the Foundation's grants, of course, were directed by original donor's terms, but the breadth of imagination of the "living hand" of the distribution committees suggests how successfully the Foundation has been a "do well" and not merely a "do good" instrument.

The Foundation blazed a trail again for American community trusts when in 1943 it created the "Combined Fund" to make it possible for modest donors to invest in philanthropy during and after their lives. The economics of trust operations, calling for constant watchfulness and inspection of investment by staffs of specially trained bankers, their attention to legal guide-lines, their perpetual consciousness of another person's interest and purpose, render it impractical or difficult to manage small sums of money. Yet by the time of the second World War it was becoming apparent to foundations everywhere that the instinct for philanthropy and its preservation had interested all kinds of people of large and small means, in one of those infrequent splendid natural spreads of the democratic idea.

The Combined Fund was made a repository for memorials and small gifts, each retaining its identity but their total amounting to sizable and manageable investment.

Without disturbance of the original trust-and-purpose resolutions, the three (at that time) multiple trustee banks enacted independent resolutions to set up this joint depository for all small gifts, bequests, and charity trusts. Two of the authors of the fund at the Cleveland Trust Company, I. F. Freiberger and A. R. Horr, immediately gave $500 each; Mrs. Malcolm L. McBride gave the trustee Central National Bank $1,000 as a memorial to her husband, who had served as member and chairman for 24 years on the Foundation Distribution Committee, and the trustee National City Bank contributed $1,000 to its fund.

This gave the Foundation a new appeal, and a good one, and the Combined Fund was a moral and material success from its start. (When the Society National Bank and Union Commerce Bank some years later adopted similar Combined Fund resolutions, Mr. and Mrs. Harold T. Clark helped to activate the Funds by $500 contributions.) Ten years later, the Combined Fund contained $146,729; in 1962 it was more than a million dollars, with nearly 1,500 separate gifts and bequests. The "memorial" opportunity has drawn 100 such life-testimonial funds; besides that to Mr. McBride, the Combined Fund has memorial gifts in honor of five other members of the Distribution Committee, and another to Director Leyton E. Carter, who was widely known and respected among the cultural and welfare population of Cleveland. It has attracted hundreds of small (and a few sizable) donors. There is a memorial fund for the long-time president of a big league baseball team, and another to one of the great baseball stars of all time, Tris Speaker. Today almost all the largest community trusts have this or similar means to accept the most modest gifts to be preserved and applied in the name of generosity.

In another development pioneer for the country, the Cleveland Foundation opened its doors to a special kind of trust of which it has now nearly a score, with eventual asset value of more than $15,000,000. These provide — in varying amounts — for payment of annuities to certain individuals prior to payment of the balance of the income to the Foundation; ultimately the whole income will go to the Foundation, and in 1962 three-fourths of the total income came to it.

These trusts were devised for those who wished to maintain both private supports and philanthropic intentions from the start. They stemmed from the original Goff philosophy noted in an earlier chapter.

Looking back over the years, these "milestones" mark the road of the Cleveland Foundation's growth:

1919 — The first income from endowment.

1927 — First endowment for education and scholarships.

1930 — The multiple trusteeship established.

1931 — The Harry Coulby Fund, bringing substantial income for child care, health, and hospital grants.

1934 — National City Bank becomes a Trustee.

1940 — The Frederick W. and Henryett Slocum Judd Fund to provide library services for the handicapped and shut-ins in their homes.

1942 — First funds for care of the needy and the aged from the Lynn J. and Eva D. Hammond Fund.

1943 — The Combined Fund is established.

1946 — Significant increase in unrestricted income for general philanthropy, not limited to specific purpose or institution, from the Frederic M. and Nettie E. Backus Fund.

1950 — Another significant increase in Foundation capital from the Crispin and Kate Oglebay Trust.

1951 — The A. E. Convers Fund, largest trust for unrestricted philanthropic distribution.

1955 — Union Commerce Bank becomes a Foundation Trustee.

1957 — Philanthropic disbursements pass $1,000,000 mark.

1959 — The Fred H. Chapin Memorial Fund provides major increase in unrestricted income.

1960 — Society National Bank adopts Foundation Resolution bringing total of trustee banks to five. Eugene S. and Blanche R. Halle Memorial Fund adds substantially to Foundation endowment.

1961 — Cleveland Foundation Library established in cooperation with Foundation Library Center of New York City. Foundation assets increase by nearly $11,000,000, a major portion by gifts from the Leonard C. Hanna, Jr. Fund.

1962 — Philanthropic disbursements pass $2,000,000 mark.

One of the highest compliments ever paid the pioneer foundation was disclosed December 18, 1961, at a civic luncheon given by the Foundation Distribution Committee. It was announced that the Ford Foundation and the Leonard C. Hanna, Jr. Fund had each made grants of $1,250,000 so that the Cleveland Foundation could form the "Greater Cleveland Associated Foundation" for the purpose of developing community programs, through problem surveys, special research, and pilot projects. In this association, five large private foundations of Cleveland joined in the sponsorship.

As the staff of the Associated Foundation was assembled under Kent H. Smith (a member of the Foundation Distribution Committee), as chairman, and Dr. James A. Norton as president, studies were under analysis for the new operation of such problems as automation and unemployment, urban life difficulties, juvenile delinquency, the settlement of new citizens, and the social aspects of urban renewal. The usefulness of as broad an agency of research as this might well stimulate the thinking of private and corporate foundations.

The Foundation in 1962 listed among its assets 13 trusts each of more than a million dollars — some of these at present paying some income to survivors but all of them eventually to be solely for the benefit of the Foundation. These are the Backus Fund of $2,148,506; George H. Boyd Fund, $1,559,251; Fred H. Chapin

Fund, $2,163,745; the Convers Fund, $5,274,078; the Coulby Fund of $3,487,694 (another Coulby Fund provides $835,311); Eugene S. and Blanche R. Halle Fund, $2,055,096; Edwin T. and Mary E. Hamilton Fund, $1,106,820; the Hammond Fund of $1,077,578; Leonard C. Hanna Jr. Cleveland Foundation Special Purpose Fund, $1,073,065; Leonard C. Hanna Jr. Community Development Fund, $5,132,234; Leonard C. Hanna Jr. Associated Foundation Trust, $2,469,122 (two other Hanna funds total more than a half million); Karamu House Trust, $1,055,258; the Oglebay Trust of $2,023,787. Seven other private trust bequests exceed a half million dollars each.

The personal histories behind these thirteen largest trusts and their estates have both similarities and curious differences. The Coulby, Hanna, and Oglebay means all came from the Great Lakes iron ore, coal, and shipping businesses; Messrs. Coulby and Oglebay were operators in separate mining and shipping companies and Mr. Hanna the heir of a prominent operator. Leonard C. Hanna, Jr., was the greatest philanthropist in Cleveland's history, his own private trusts having distributed many millions to the art, music, culture, and education of the community.

Mr. Coulby, born in England, came to Cleveland as a youth, studied shorthand, and was private secretary, in his twenties, to John Hay, later Secretary of State and ambassador. His business connections led to Coulby's initiation into the ore and shipping partnership of Pickands Mather & Co. He became the most influential single figure in the organization of the lakes traffic for the steel industry.

Mr. Oglebay's trust agreement has been described as setting down his "whole philosophy of life and his philosophy regarding the disposition of wealth." He expressed a preference that the Foundation employ half of the trust income to support community activities at Oglebay Park, Wheeling's great forest, sport, and nature reserve given to that city by Mr. Oglebay's uncle and of which the nephew became a guardian and patron. He expressed another preference that most of the rest of the income go to support the Western Reserve University School of Medicine.

The Backus fortune came from the earliest days of the oil business. The fund was created by Bertha E. Backus Hale as a memorial to her parents, Frederic M. and Nettie E. Backus, and years after Mrs. Hale no longer lived in Cleveland. It was the first large trust whose income was unrestricted, making its acquisition in 1946 a milestone indeed.

The Judd trust, likewise noted as a "milestone," was accumulated by a one-time skilled machine tool worker who eventually built his own company. Both Mr. and Mrs. Judd lived lives which could be defined as pleasant and comfortable, both died without periods of invalidism; the noteworthy character of their trust purpose is that income should be distributed to bring the services of the Cleveland Public Library to invalids and shut-ins.

With this income, the library since 1941 has delivered more than 2,000,000 books to more than 500,000 isolated readers and has circulated tens of thousands of pictures, slides, and films to individuals, nursing homes, and hospitals — each with a specially designed "Judd" bookplate.

The estate of Fred H. Chapin, machine tool manufacturer, came to the Foundation on the basis of his personal observation of the Foundation's work as a member of the Distribution Committee for eight years. The fund is not restricted as to purpose.

Eugene S. Halle, a founder of the Cleveland Stock Exchange, was one of Cleveland's leading philanthropists. Gifts from the Halle Fund are divided equally between Jewish and non-Jewish organizations.

One of the smaller trusts the Foundation regards as one of its most exemplary and famous: it has a current value of about $10,000 (originally $7,752) and it was bestowed into the hands of the Foundation in 1949 by Miss Katherine Bohm, a German-born laundress for all of her long life in Cleveland. She died in modest quarters at the age of 80, almost blind and having had one leg amputated; she left her life savings to be distributed as the Foundation saw fit, although how she knew of the Foundation and discerned its principal purpose remains a mystery. The Foundation used the first income from this bequest for eye and dental work for persons needing such to get employment.

Twenty-six men and women from the most prominent walks of life have served as Distribution Committee members during the Foundation's half century. Their average term has been nine and a half years; the longest was 24, two others 18. The following roster of this uncompensated civic and guardian duty includes present members.

MEMBERS OF DISTRIBUTION COMMITTEE
AND YEARS OF SERVICE

James D. Williamson, Chairman (1917-1922)	1917-22
Thomas G. Fitzsimons	1917-21
Miss Belle Sherwin	1917-24
Ambrose Swasey	1917-19
Malcolm L. McBride, Chairman (1922-1941)	1917-41
William H. Prescott	1919-31
Thomas L. Johnson	1921-26
Leonard P. Ayres	1922-40
Mrs. F. H. Goff	1924-42
Carl W. Brand, Chairman (1942)	1926-42
Henry G. Dalton	1931-39
Fred S. McConnell, Chairman (1942-1955)	1939-55
Joseph C. Hostetler	1940-42
Mrs. Benjamin P. Bole	1942-47
Nap. H. Boynton	1942-49
Harold T. Clark	1942-56
William E. Wickenden	1942-47
Mrs. Robert H. Bishop, Jr.	1947-57
John L. McChord, Chairman (1955-1956)	1947-56
Fred H. Chapin	1950-58
Ellwood H. Fisher, Chairman (1956-1962)	1955-
John A. Greene	1956-61
John C. Virden	1956-
Kent H. Smith	1958-
Mrs. Royal Firman, Jr.	1958-
John Sherwin, Chairman (1963-)	1961-

By odd circumstance, the five women members all were named by different mayors of Cleveland, perhaps because Mayor Harry L. Davis fixed a precedent in selecting Miss Sherwin. Some mayors made their own selections, a few asked for nominee suggestions. The various senior federal and probate judges sometimes have asked not only the Foundation but other civic institutions for suggestions, although one jurist looked upon his appointing responsibility so seriously as to have it seem a risk of discretion to make any suggestion.

Twenty-six members in fifty years indicates how fluid the system of selection has become, for this means a new member of the committee on the average of every two years.

Members of the Trustees Committee serve by virtue of their executive positions at each of the trustee banks. Present members of this Committee are: George Gund, chairman of board, Cleveland Trust Company, who is chairman of Trustees Committee; Francis H. Beam, chairman of board, The National City Bank of Cleveland; Mervin B. France, president, Society National Bank of Cleveland; George R. Herzog, chairman of board, Union Commerce Bank and James J. Nance, president, Central National Bank of Cleveland.

The list of directors of the Foundation is short in comparison with the roster of the Distribution Committee. There have been but four in fifty years.

Carlton K. Matson succeeded Raymond Moley as director in 1924. He came from newspaper and advertising fields and had been head of the Cleveland Trust Company public relations. He might be remembered as the director who made the most speeches and wrote the most descriptions of the Foundation's attractions to Cleveland and to other communities. In 1928 he resigned to take a metropolitan newspaper editorship (which led him shortly to the directorship of the Buffalo Foundation for two years) and returned to Cleveland to become a greatly admired chief editorial writer of the Cleveland Press. He died in 1948.

His successor as Foundation director in 1928 was Leyton E. Carter, whose career had included service with the Municipal Research Bureau of Cleveland and the faculties of two colleges. Mr. Carter had wide knowledge of the sciences of municipal government, and was vice chairman of a state schools survey in 1932 and chairman of the urban problems committee of the U. S. Chamber of Commerce in 1942. The tempo of the Foundation's expansion accelerated during his 25 years as director; his untimely death occurred in 1953.

Fourth and present director of the Foundation is J. Kimball Johnson, born in Chicago and educated in metallurgy and engineering at Case Institute of Technology. Following 15 years as a civil and sanitary engineer in this country and Cuba, Mr. Johnson became immersed in government and sociology as a pioneer in the first Social Security Administration and the U. S. Employment Service. His planning and improvising sagacity for human relief during the 1930 depression years led to his becoming a regional director of the

World War II manpower mobilization. During his years as director, the Foundation's greatest growth has occurred.

Miss Dorothy Ruth, who has been administrative aide to Directors Carter and Johnson, was also appointed assistant secretary of the Foundation in 1956. She is a graduate of Flora Stone Mather College of Western Reserve University and served as president of that Alumnae Association in 1961.

CHAPTER V

The Foundations' Impact of Today

EVEN in a civilization growing accustomed to billions of public and private expenditure and trillions of space-miles, the annual total of $16,750,000 given to charitable, community, social welfare, health and research benefits is a figure at which to look twice. This was the 1962 distribution of grants by the more than 180 community trusts reporting to the National Council. A decade of philanthropic spending at this rate has real impact on today's American living. But, thanks to the vigilance of community foundation guardianship between trustee banks and public-service distribution boards, this has steadily been an increasing statistic, and will continue to rise at something akin to arithmetic progression. The vault of these desirable benefits has no actual ceiling.

The total active capital reported by these community trusts in 1962 was approximately $423,000,000 — likewise a record of steady increase, as more and more donors realize the philosophy of thwarting the "dead hand," and more and more foundations impress their communities with their potential for good works. The rise of this total in two years was over $60,000,000; the increase in one year in the number of active trusts reporting was twenty. Twenty-two new community foundations were organized in the previous 24 months.

Some forty foundations had more than $1,000,000 in capital (eight of them went above the $1,000,000 mark in 1961).

Based upon 1962 preliminary reports, following is a list of the largest community foundations with the amount of their philanthropic disbursements for that year. Assets are reported at market value of active capital except where (L) appears denoting ledger value.

Name	Assets	Philanthropic Disbursements
Cleveland Foundation	$65,247,279	$2,260,766
New York Community Trust	50,460,000	2,559,000
Committee of the Permanent Charity Fund (Boston)	46,431,527	1,649,770
Chicago Community Trust	45,088,705	1,563,660
Hartford Foundation for Public Giving	22,351,681	409,617
Kalamazoo Foundation	22,302,000	305,300
New Haven Foundation	16,623,000	498,822
California Community Foundation	14,666,272	405,124
Winston-Salem Foundation	12,701,329	332,822
Pittsburgh Foundation	12,399,524	576,027
Indianapolis Foundation	11,766,057	370,359
Grand Rapids Foundation	6,950,759 (L)	231,806
Winnipeg Foundation	6,577,976	274,828
Philadelphia Foundation	6,300,000	488,000
Rhode Island Foundation	5,932,716	202,826
Buffalo Foundation	5,810,510	182,720
Vancouver Foundation	5,500,000	288,629
Minneapolis Foundation	5,282,000	133,214
San Francisco Foundation	4,724,967	583,995

Ohio leads the country in the number of community foundations with 19; there are 15 in Michigan, 12 in Pennsylvania, ten in Illinois, and eight each in New York, Massachusetts, Indiana, and California. There are six in Canada — at Winnipeg, Hamilton, Calgary, London, Victoria, and Vancouver. One of the newest, the New Hampshire Charitable Fund (with the chief justice of the state supreme court as member of its distribution committee), covers a whole state; two, Amarillo Area Foundation and Fargo Moorhead Area Foundation, cross state lines in their territory.

Of the philanthropy distributed, the great bulk is from income, although the exact proportion will vary from year to year with the exigencies of old and new trusts respectively going and coming which put a time limit on distribution of principal. A majority of community trusts reported, in toto, in 1960 that 74.5 percent of the distribution was from income and 25.5 from principal; in 1961, it was 81.1 percent income and 18.9 principal.

No writer of fiction could devise the details of some of the curious, sentimental, and imaginative benefactions which community trust committees and staffs are executing under terms of various trusts and designated funds. Some of these are famous in the lore of trust bankers, foundation distributors, and lawyers. James Dean and his wife for many years enjoyed yachting on their "Skookum," and to them the old Boston Light was symbol and institution, so that for years they sailed to it each Sunday morning carrying Boston Sunday newspapers to the isolated lighthouse crew — it was a place to sail and to cement seafaring friendship.

Mr. Dean left a special fund of $10,000 to the Boston Committee of the Permanent Charity Fund to perpetuate this Sunday delivery "of no more than four different Boston Sunday newspapers," and since 1946, from April to November, the Boston Fund has delivered the papers just as the Deans did. And the Boston Light has become the engraved and printed "masthead" of the Boston Fund.

Every year the New York Community Trust finances the town fair of the tiny community of St. James, in the Missouri Ozarks, and sees that the fair maintains prize competitions for the best quilts and the best women's dresses made from flour and farm sacks; this under the instruction of the Lucy Wortham James trust set up for philanthropy in the village where her grandfather had an iron works in 1826 which was the foundation of three generations of an iron and ore fortune. St. James has a model modern library and a recreation park from the trust. But the best part of this story begins with the "company doctor" of the iron works who brought Lucy Wortham James into the world, Dr. Samuel H. Headlee; the niece with whom he lived, when she died, sent the New York Community Trust a cocoa tin containing $1,080 in currency and a note asking that this be added to Miss James' philanthropy for St. James, Missouri. Among other benefactions, Miss Headlee's bequest has furnished andirons for the model library and a bible for the Episcopal church of the village.

It was during World War II, and the 1940 "blitz" of London, that thirteen New York litterateurs followed the lead of Frank Morley in amassing $1,300 to preserve from the air attacks a bust of Mrs. Samuel Pepys and the bells of St. Bartholomew the Great. The late James Thurber, John Mason Brown, and Russel Crouse were among them; the $1,300 was committed to the New York trust to do the best it could toward these objectives. With other available funds, the Community Trust this many years later has preserved a century-old tide mill, the last corn mill in England, and the seafarers' church of All Hallows Barking-by-the-Tower, besides the original objectives.

The very first donor to the New York Trust was Mrs. Rosebel G. Schiff, who in 1924 set up $1,000 in memory of a beloved public school principal, Miss Teresa E. Bernholtz of Public School No. 9. Each year, a prize in the name of Miss Bernholtz goes to the girl of that school who "has earned the highest respect of her teachers" and the Trust is ready to continue the award, under "cy pres" (legal term for "as near as possible"), after Public School No. 9 is no more, in order to keep Miss Bernholtz's memory green.

All the zoos in New York and Brooklyn have wheel chairs, with attendants, for crippled and arthritic visitors thanks to the trust fund of Mr. and Mrs. Herbert L. Griggs; Mrs. Griggs was an invalid from arthritis. But she and Mr. Griggs, a Manhattan banker, were less interested in medical research than in trying to alleviate the painful lives of arthritics; their $300,000 fund through various agencies and institutions has financed special appliances, food, transport, and delights — including "arthritic" shoes — for sufferers, as the New York Community Trust has carried out the designation.

Around New York are markers of spots of history in bronze and aluminum tablets which have been studied, selected, and installed by the New York Trust from a Fund by Mrs. Andrew C. McKenzie, an architect's relict who wished something appropriate to the physical city; and once a year young artists of the Metropolitan Opera perform before a suitable board of judges for rewards of "assistance to young artists" from a fund the Trust executes from the late Anna E. Schoen-Rene, singer and teacher of the opera.

New York Community Trust exceeded all in geography and breadth of its distribution in 1961; to 643 organizations in 159 cities in 28 states and eight foreign countries.

Twelve banks of New York and Westchester are trustees of the New York Community Trust. The Trust created an affiliate "Community Funds, Inc." to accept, manage, and invest moderate funds and donations, within which is another auxiliary, "The Common Wealth," to which bequests of as little as $500 may be made and for which four New York savings banks accept specific accounts which are turned over to "The Common Wealth" fund when they reach $500, or on the donor's death. Some of these savings accounts accumulate at the rate of a few dollars a week.

Director Hayes has within physical vision, so to speak, one of the most glittering examples of the "dead hand," the Randall "Snug Harbor" home for retired seamen on Staten Island. Founded in 1801, it now shelters a dwindling number of seafaring claimants (because of this day of pensions for sailors, too), with assets of $120,000,000 which courts for years have kept segregated and idle because of the trust set up for a single purpose by Robert Richard Randall. Had a community foundation been available to Randall at the turn of the nineteenth century, his farm property today would be translated into hundreds of millions of dollars for philanthropy far beyond his generous intention.

Occasionally the New York Community Trust publishes a story about the operation of some of its trusts, the latest of which describes a scholar's purpose that great teaching and scholarship not be forgot. This is the memorial fund of Lane Cooper, distinguished professor emeritus of English at Cornell University for 57 years. The fund amounts to about a half million dollars; its income is to provide scholarships or eventually other welfare, for upperclass undergraduates in the humanities. It stipulates that the beneficiaries learn something of the lives of Professor Cooper's father, who was a Rutgers professor of Greek, and of Professor Albert Stanburrough Cook, a student of the elder Cooper and a teacher at Yale of the son.

Lane Cooper wrote of his purpose: "I have watched great gifts of money go to the erection of educational buildings, smaller gifts to salaries for teachers, and the smallest to the protection and fostering of exceptional talent among the students. It is to the talented but impecunious students that gifts should go first of all."

A triumph over the "dead hand" of which Mr. Hayes is proud is the Community Trust's administration of a $17,000 fund originally raised to teach lace making and commerce to Indian women on American reservations — which now provides scholarships for Indian boys and girls all over the country.

Chicago Community Trust's capital in 1962 was $45,088,705 and its distribution $1,563,660, in 1960, the Elizabeth McCormick Memorial Fund of nearly $4,000,000 was placed in its hands after 53 years of family trustee management. James Brown IV, executive director of the Chicago Trust, had also served as a trustee of the McCormick Fund.

The stories behind some of the larger Chicago trust funds, as told by Frank Loomis, long-time Chicago Community Trust director now retired, are full of the "human interest" of human impulse. The Harry B. Lusch fund, now $2,000,000, came from an individual who farmed into modern times in a corner of Chicago's municipal area, and who became rich from a talent for renovating all kinds of properties. His bequest involved the improvement of waste timber lands in Arkansas out of which social and welfare agencies of Chicago derive income today. A grandson of the man for whom Cook County was named, William J. Cook, left in the Trust's hands an estate of $592,899 now grown to nearly $3,000,000, from which probably the greatest number of college scholarships for high school pupils in any city of the land now come; 439 had been granted up to 1961.

An invalid bachelor, George Firmenich, who "read in the papers" and then consulted friends over several years, turned over an estate lately valued at $3,396,392. A doctor turned to the Community Trust for administration of funds for medical education and research, then interested his doctor brother, and the William Allen Pusey and Brown Pusey bequest stands at $375,000.

A one-time "poor farm boy" whose instinct was to help other poor farm boys (there are not so many of his kind in America today) created the powerful WLS radio station and made a bequest of a large interest in it, which, when the station was sold, brought the Chicago Trust $3,695,593. He was Burridge D. Butler, and Mrs. Butler's estate added more than a half million.

A chairman of Inland Steel Corporation, George Herbert Jones, set up a fund in the Trust of $1,427,925, and when he bequeathed the bulk of his worth to his daughter, Mrs. Ruth Jones Allison, he recommended the Community Trust for her ultimate disposition. Mrs. Allison agreed and left in the Trust's hands a fund of $4,771,147; it was she, active in Americanization work, who had first told her father about the Community Trust.

One of the great Chicago Trust leaders was Clifford W. Barnes, the former president of Illinois College who had helped Mr. Harris launch the Chicago foundation and became the first chairman of its executive committee.

He served in this post for 28 years; he and Mrs. Barnes left to it a fund of $672,250.

Mrs. Charles H. Worcester was for years a principal supporter of the Chicago Convalescent Home for Women and Children; there came a time when she and the board of the Home decided to discontinue its work, and in 1948 the property was turned over to the Community Trust because of the interest and counsel it had maintained. Most of the estates of Mr. and Mrs. Worcester came to the Community Trust in 1955, their value $1,620,391.

Chicago has a "Combined Fund" through an establishment by six of its trustees to accept gifts of any size up to $10,000 for individual identification and intent and joint management and investment. In 1958, the first woman member of the Chicago Community Trust executive committee was named, Mrs. C. Philip Miller.

Transformation and enlargement of the work of the Boston Committee of the Permanent Charity Fund after 1960 because of the record bequest of the Albert Stone, Jr., $19,000,000 trust is one of the most unusual chapters of the community foundations' story. Until the Stone gift, the Fund had restricted its grants to charitable and welfare agencies. It has broadened these today into additional cultural and civic benefactions and capital gifts to colleges and institutions.

The dramatic aura around Mr. Stone's bequest (and his sister's additional trust fund) extends over his identity and personality. Newspapers reporting the bequest headlined him as a "Mystery Financier," and the Fund had no previous intimation of this all-time largest foundation windfall. Stone had been a depositor of the Boston Safe Deposit & Trust for many years, but rarely visited the bank and it knew little about him. Twenty years before his bequest, he walked into the Boston Fund office one day to ask just what it "did for charity," and thereafter was an annual donor through the office to the Boston United Fund. President William W. Wolbach of the bank said he knew Mr. Stone slightly as a "gracious, warm-hearted, retiring" man of "great dignity." But even the antecedents of this considerable fortune were not entirely defined.

Born in 1878 of midwestern parents who settled in Boston, Stone attended Chauncy Hall School but no college. He had an inheritance of substantial amount; he made coal and textile investments, but his principal business was in commercial and industrial real estate. He and his sister lived somewhat as recluses in a Victorian-style family home for 60 years.

One of the recent "cultural" gifts of the Permanent Charity Fund was $35,000 to the Boston Opera Association toward an auditorium in Boston's new Prudential Center suitable for opera and ballet.

According to Director Bender — a former Harvard dean — the outstanding Boston Fund total help to hospitals reflects the heavy concentration in that area of university-connected private teaching hospitals. Two of its current college grants (Harvard and Tufts) are intended to help their renewal of their areas. One grant to Harvard in 1961 was for wide study of how to coordinate hospital teaching.

Over two years, the Fund has given more than $100,000 to the Action for Boston Community Development concerned with humane problems of the "core city," which launched this movement now substantially supported by a five-year Ford Foundation grant; and anticipates investing a great deal more in this and allied urban renewal programs. Within this stimulation is neighborhoods' participation in renewal.

Two policy characteristics of the Boston Fund: It does not support any medical or scientific research because it "is not equipped to evaluate the relative quality and significance of individual scientific research projects, and there is so much money available for these purposes from governmental and other sources. . ." It does use "a significant part of its income" contributing to operating costs of tested agencies. Some foundations (notably Pittsburgh) do not grant funds for operating budgets; some do make grants for medical and at least quasi-scientific research.

Judges appoint four of the members of the Boston Fund's incorporated Distribution Committee, the trustee bank three.

The Pittsburgh Foundation in 1961 had 93 funds valued at more than $13,000,000. Its grants emphasized programs of research, demonstration, and experiment in social, health, medical, and educational fields. Its two largest funds, each in excess of $2,000,000, were created by Harry Wherrett, president of Pittsburgh Plate Glass Co., and William M. Knox of New Castle, Pa. It administers special purpose funds for scholarship aid, child care, fuel for the needy, girls' vocational training, care of the aged, eyeglasses for persons on public assistance, help for opera singers and art students, nature and history museum extension, lecture courses, improvement of public education, social work, journalism, aviation safety, and secondary school honors. It has awarded travel and study benefits, bought equipment for group work agencies, and — in a community famous for carrying out modern physical urban planning into action — subsidized a number of planning projects.

Philadelphia Foundation made a total distribution in 1962 of nearly $500,000, or more than double that of only four years before, when it was made into an actual community trust. The largest single fund is the William J. McCahan III Fund, over which the Distribution Committee has full discretion but with prior considerations requested. Totaling about $5,500,000, it came to the Foundation in 1961. One special purpose fund in the Philadelphia Foundation appears unlike any other grant recorded; it provides summer day-camp trips for indigent elderly citizens.

In the Connecticut cities of New Haven and Hartford are two foundations which are exemplary among mid-sized American municipalities for proportion and growth. The Hartford Foundation for Public Giving has capital of $22,352,000 and in 1962 distributed $409,617 in benefactions. The New Haven Foundation had capital of $16,623,000 and made grants of $498,822 in 1962. Both stem from change in state law in 1925 to permit designations in wills to community trusts. This had been developed largely by a small group of New Haven bankers and lawyers, notably Thomas M. Steele, Osborne A. Day, and James Dwight Dana.

The Corporate Fiduciaries Association of the New Haven banks organized the New Haven Foundation. It received the Silverthau Fund in 1942 — worth more than a million dollars now — which proposed that the Distribution Committee use what it thought wise of the income to supply the New Haven poor with milk and coal. While the committee has faithfully applied funds to this intention, the income grew so steadily that the primary purpose is a small philanthropy today compared to what the Silverthau Fund accomplishes elsewhere.

Two brothers, Frank and Ross Gates of Derby — a town originally outside the geographical limits of the Foundation — created the largest trusts in the New Haven Foundation, amounting today to about half the book value of all funds, somewhat less in market value. The Gates brothers were unsuspected as potential donors; they learned of the Foundation through one of the trustee banks. In 1948, the trustee banks established a "general fund" which has drawn thousands of smaller philanthropic gifts, principally memorial funds; obituary notices in the New Haven newspapers frequently suggest the "general fund" to friends of the deceased. In Foundation grants, three colleges, including Yale, have benefited, and arts festivals and "pops" concerts been supported; in 1962, the Foundation has supported a study of family problems in restricted neighborhoods.

Hartford Foundation for Public Giving was conceived in the early 1920's — looking forward to the beneficient change in the state law — by two bank trust officers, Maynard T. Hazen of the United States Security Trust Co. and Clark T. Durant of Hartford-Connecticut Trust Co. They drafted resolutions for their institutions to adopt in 1925. Both had watched with interest the Goff development in Cleveland; both had known of perpetual charitable bequests which had failed because of changed conditions.

It was not until 1934, however, that the two banks created a Distribution Committee of four citizens appointed by two judges, the mayor, and the president of the Community Chest and three named by the trustees (appointing authority later was given the president of Trinity College also). The initial distribution, in 1936, was of $982; it went for a study of parental education related to juvenile delinquency. A mere 25 years later the Foundation was disbursing more than half a million.

John M. K. Davis, Chairman of the Distribution Committee, has served as a member of that committee since its inception in 1934. His devoted efforts in the development of the Foundation were given an assist when Russell T. Foster was appointed in 1954 as the first full time executive.

Largest trust administered by Hartford Foundation is the Howard H. Garmany estate listed in 1962 at $7,411,664 but estimated to be close to thirteen millions at market value. Three other trusts exceed a million. Hartford offers a "combined fund" for individual gifts of $100 or more, with a current rising and respectable total.

Besides its aforementioned gifts to establish a central building for city community welfare and charity services, Hartford Foundation in 1962 made large grants to three colleges, $50,000 for educational TV, more than $100,000 to hospitals and health care. Among other fund assignments in recent years were those to the city's symphony, Junior Achievement, Little League baseball, prisoner rehabilitation, and graduate fellowships in science and social work study.

The chairman of the Distribution Committee of the San Francisco Foundation is the creator of the largest single trust in the Foundation's operations, the $1,375,000 William H. and Ethel W. Crocker memorial fund by Mrs. Henry Potter Russell, their daughter. Being distributed to the Foundation currently is the Doris Martin Miller Trust, anticipated to exceed a million dollars, whose income is marked for hospital and surgical care of indigent cancer sufferers. As Director John R. May puts it, "when and if cancer is conquered," such a fund, in perpetuity, might have a very broad effectiveness in many directions. A third trust in the San Francisco Foundation is the William R. and Agnes H. McGuire fund, its income preferably for the help of handicapped children, the aged, and the blind. This bequest was made to the Foundation a few years ago by a lonely widow in her 90's. Among the beneficiaries of the Foundation are programs for the aid of mental disorder and alcohol victims. It was the solemn judgment of the San Francisco Foundation committee that a harpsichord for a music school and a male giraffe for the city's zoo, to encourage progeny, were good dispositions of some of its unrestricted funds.

The San Francisco Foundation reported in 1962 capital of $4,725,000 and a distribution of nearly $600,000.

A notable case of growth in a short time is that of Akron Community Trusts, which came into being in 1955 when Edwin C. Shaw left the residue of his estate in order to make foundation operation possible, and which in 1961 reported active capital of $1,562,550 and distributions of nearly $100,000, with emphasis on grants for community planning.

Trustee banks of the Metropolitan Foundation of Atlanta, established in 1951 with a multiple trustee-ship, have financed its operations for a five-year period; it succeeded and expanded an original single-trustee Atlanta Foundation begun in 1921 which did not progress rapidly. The Metropolitan Foundation trustees incorporated its Distribution Committee to be able to handle real estate gifts. It has given Atlanta's community services new support, has established a full time directorship with the appointment of A. B. Padgett, and is now beneficiary of a large number of wills.

The Woods Charitable Fund of Lincoln, Neb., spear-headed the Lincoln Foundation so a family's funds might be perpetually protected and useful. Frank H. Woods of the family in Chicago, who is also an officer of the National Council on Community Foundations, had been impressed by the functioning of the Chicago Community Trust.

This impetus to transfer family trusts to the proven longer-term protection of community foundation operation exposes a field in which the foundations may render more and more service in years to come. As mentioned, it was in Chicago also that the sizable Elizabeth McCormick private foundation was deposited into the care of the Chicago Community Trust — as many years earlier the Laura Spelman Rockefeller foundation turned for guardianship to the New York Community Trust.

One of Chicago Community Trust's most vigorous chairmen, Edward L. Ryerson, said in an address in 1947 in Cleveland:

"A phase of community trust practice generally overlooked is the growing volume of family charity trusts or foundations — of course, primarily due to the tax equation involved, but with advantages outside the tax feature. In numerous instances, they result in continuing support for useful charitable purposes which otherwise might be subjected to the ups and downs of individual income and changing viewpoints.

"On the other hand, there is grave danger of such individual trusts falling into the hands of uninformed successor trustees or bank trustees . . . of limited knowledge or individual whims . . . These personal foundations can be channeled in part if not completely through the community trust committee, and thereby give the individual grantor the satisfaction of a better way to dispense such funds and insure their maximum usefulness for all the years to come."

F. Emerson Andrews, director of the Foundation Library Center and an authority on philanthropy, reports that education is the most favored field in grants by all American foundations. Distribution of the community foundation millions departs from this pattern in that the major portion goes to social welfare with education and health following in that order according to a recent tabulation. All of the large community foundations annually support some form of community health-welfare planning. Hospitals in every city with a foundation are assisted practically on an annual basis. Probably the greatest current hospital benefaction is that of Boston's Permanent Charity Fund, with more than $700,000 distributed in the last two years for all hospital purposes. Columbus' united hospital expansion drive was spearheaded by $422,000 from the Columbus Foundation. Nearly $4,000,000 has been devoted to support of hospitals and health projects by the Cleveland Foundation in the past 40 years.

Education is undoubtedly the second largest classification of community trust distributions, if gifts for research to colleges and scholarships to individuals are included. There is hardly a community trust in the United States that does not have funds for scholarship help.

Study of the country-wide breakdown of community foundations' distributions brings to light a unique usefulness of one of their purposes, rather rare in organized benevolent dispensation: the giving of funds to churches and religious bodies per the desires of individual donors.

While in the total of all present philanthropy in the nation a very large percentage goes to churches and sectarian religion, the fact is that most private foundations — corporate, industrial, personal, — do not distribute to sectarian agencies. Practical reasons involved are from a natural democratic sentimentality, defense against a multitude of inevitable appeals, and possible corporate or legal complications.

On the other hand, the community foundations exist on pledges to carry out, as long as practical and prudent, the intentions and preferences of donors including religious benefactions. In 1961, almost 5 percent of Pittsburgh Foundation's distribution went to churches and religious bodies, and funds were distributed to churches and sectarian organizations by Chicago Community Trust, Philadelphia Foundation, and a number of others.

Several large-city foundations have committed important funds to fighting juvenile delinquency. Boston's study of delinquency and its causes has attracted national attention. The Chicago Community Trust makes grants to a large number of agencies seeking delinquency reforms, and several years ago the San Francisco Foundation set up a psychiatric clinic for the courts dealing with delinquency cases.

At least four metropolitan community trusts support educational television. The Cleveland Foundation has recently financed a community group which hopes to bring the first educational TV station to that city. The Pittsburgh Foundation finances certain programs. "Operation Alphabet," aimed at adult illiteracy, has been helped for two years by the Philadelphia Foundation, with the gratifying result that a private fund joined to put the 1962 lessons on video tape; and the Boston Permanent Charity Fund gave $75,000 to help rebuild a pioneer educational TV station after a damaging fire.

Grants are numerous for work to rehabilitate prisoners on leaving confinement. One-year Indianapolis Foundation investment in this work was $11,000; Pittsburgh and San Francisco Foundations give substantial support through special agencies; Chicago's interest in prisoner care and treatment has been lively and intermittent ever since its notable survey of the old "Bridewell" of 1922.

Many community trusts make grants for music, either its creation or education for it. More than 25 music schools of the land, and numerous symphony and philharmonic orchestras benefit from community foundations. The Columbus Foundation manages the city's symphony endowment. New Haven Foundation has discovered its symphony orchestra attracted more expressions of donor preference than any other organization.

Indianapolis assists two orchestras, and the foundations of Philadelphia, Pittsburgh, Cleveland, San Francisco, and Chicago have given many thousands to the noted symphony establishments of each. In a single year, New York Community Trust has made grants to the opera, several orchestras (including whole concert series), and a dozen schools of music.

Some foundations have gone all out to give modern office homes to their cities' organized charities. The Indianapolis Foundation in 1953, at a cost of nearly two million dollars, completed a building for the city's United Fund and 35 of its agencies, carrying out the intent of an affiliate, the William E. English Foundation. Jack Killen serves as executive of both foundations and "manages" the building. New Haven Foundation has contributed more than a half million dollars toward a projected charity agency headquarters building, and the Hartford Foundation made a $100,000 grant to a United Fund-agencies headquarters building.

The Oshkosh Foundation, in a bequest of more than $1,000,000 in 1959, was made depositary for nearly $150,000 of the trust to be applied to a new Y.M.C.A. building.

One "surprise" element in the maturing of foundations across the country is the emergence without warning of support from people of modest means in the best democratic tradition. The Cleveland laundress whose life savings were contributed unrestricted had a counterpart in Mrs. Josephine Eutenauer of Seattle who left $29,000 "for the benefit of Seattle" to the Seattle Foundation, which was similarly unaware of her existence. In Columbus, a linotype operator setting into type in the printing shop the story of the Columbus Foundation was moved to make a will leaving $500 to it — which today furnishes a continuous shelf of books on printing and publishing in the Columbus Public Library. An assistant at the same library left a surprise gift of $350,000 to the Foundation after her death. Most later-date foundations have by now had the thrilling experience of not entirely expected bequests of proportions sufficient to "put them in business." For example, within the last two years, a $300,000 bequest to the Greater Lansing (Mich.) Foundation by Ray Potter, banker; the income from half of a $2,000,000 estate of Charles F. Burroughs to the Norfolk (Va.) Foundation; a $300,000 bequest to the Greenville County (S.C.) Foundation by W. N. Watson, Jr. To the smaller city community trusts these have the galvanizing effects that a Boston Stone or Cleveland Hanna trust can produce: to the foundation's originators, enthusiasts, and directors, this is acceptance and success.

Among large and small communities, there is the same variety of dimensions to what a foundation can do that will be urgent and popular. In Oshkosh, Wis., and Portland, Ind., badly needed public swimming baths did not materialize until the Oshkosh and Portland County Foundations respectively led public campaigns for them. The Greenville County (S.C.) Foundation struck wide response when it funded a $20,000 engineering study for needed expansion of the city's services, and so did the Spartanburg County Foundation, in adjacent territory, with a $25,000 survey of the county's health and welfare needs and present services. The Thomasville (N.C.) Foundation projected and led a community clean-up campaign.

Norfolk's fine library is the result of the Norfolk Foundation's large gift and public leadership.

The "dead hand" could surely be said to have been defeated in such modern grants as that by the Winnipeg Foundation to Manitoba's largest teaching hospital for an LGP30 Digital Computer for making mathematical analyses of data in the Department of Electroencephalography; or those by the Philadelphia Foundation for tandem bikes on which the blind can partner with a seeing pilot, and for a promotional parks-museum bus line.

A number of community trusts make their managerial, investigative, and distribution services available to private and corporation foundations, as an indirect result of the considerable growth of private philanthropies in the years since Congress authorized tax exemption for charitable gifts. An instance is the Philadelphia Foundation's administration of the Hortense Loeb Fund in a bank not a trustee of the Philadelphia Foundation. The Loeb fund's purpose was to distribute income and principal to institutions for child care and welfare, and its guardians asked the Foundation to set up a project related to children in multi-problem families. The Foundation administers it at the rate of $100,000 a year among several child care agencies, the Health and Welfare Council, and University of Pennsylvania School of Social Work.

Director Hayes of the New York Community Trust, which has accepted about $1,000,000 from corporations for administration and disbursed a large part of it, has pointed out that community trust services for a company or private fund mean responsible handling and accounting, verified and orderly programs for grants, an evenness of financial level in the "foundation reservoir," and insurance of the tax-free status of these corporation funds as long as they are in foundation hands. The Detroit Community Trust (through the United Metropolitan Community Services) makes grants for the J. L. Hudson Co. and the Easlinger-Misch Co. foundations; the Buffalo Foundation for charitable funds set up by two Buffalo department stores.

"Consult and Advise Funds" is what this extension of service is termed by the San Francisco Foundation, which handles distributions for private and corporate funds at a fixed fee for such service. Company foundations it serves include the Doran Co. of California, Levi Strauss and Co., and 14 personal and family foundations. The Mount Vernon (O.) Community Trust, in a rural Ohio county, expends a quarter of its total services on corporate funds, and company foundation management is aided by the Pittsburgh Foundation, New Haven Foundation, and Spartanburg (S.C.) County Foundation. The Junior League Fund of Columbus is administered by the Columbus Foundation. These services are furnished at a small fee charged by the community foundation.

Some of the "best jobs" by community foundations for their communities are hardly to be measured in dollars. These include the vitalization of Chicago's Community Chest by the Chicago Community Trust; the Minneapolis Foundation's setting up first real communication and co-ordination of that city's family foundations, lifting the level of local philanthropy; the Buffalo Foundation's organization of its city's social welfare agencies into federation and the creation of an area-wide child welfare council. Under the direction of Mrs. Jane W. Skinner, executive secretary, the Foundation has also carried on a major scholarship program for Buffalo students.

In recent months, the Boston Fund has reorganized and re-located work of a number of family service agencies. Back in 1944, the Boston Fund supported a survey into state welfare services for children. Some overhaul of public services was achieved, and a valuable manual of procedures dealing with guardianships in the Massachusetts Department of Welfare was produced.

In every city, town, or county in which they are located, the community foundations regularly are "news" to their newspapers, radio, and TV stations. The unqualified purpose of all community trusts, since the beginning in Cleveland, to make entirely public their status, progress, distributions, and operations converted them into a new kind of public agency to be closely reported by the media; and the humane character of their grants, with their overtones of "human interest," to say nothing of the frequent challenges by the foundations to their community imaginations, has kept the public frankly and cordially informed and acquainted.

The Saint Paul Foundation maintains a weekly advertising campaign the year round in its city's newspapers, with an additional advertisement of its operation and resources in one Sunday paper per month. Director

Louis S. Headley, former banker and lawyer, served for a number of years as president of the National Council on Community Foundations. The Lincoln (Neb.) Foundation periodically advertises its "Book of Memory" — based on the appeal of memorial trusts — in newspapers, and the Hamilton (Ont.) Foundation uses newspaper advertising to its benefit. The Cleveland, Hartford, New Haven and Pittsburgh Foundations once a year employ full page newspaper advertisements for the annual report of their funds and grants. In their early days, the larger foundations used promotional newspaper advertising for growth purposes, but their advertising today is rare.

* * *

It is more than likely that, for all the splendor of his vision, Fred Goff could not have anticipated the number, the wealth, and the horizons of the community foundations of today. The world of 1914 into which he introduced his concept could never have imagined the immense broadening of so many of the elements of modern foundation functioning; the onrush of knowledge and discovery in science and the social systems, the changes in history and tax laws, the acceleration of the accumulation of means, the newer assumptions of social consciousness. All of these have worked to point up the Goff philosophy, but to degrees and with intensities he in his day could hardly have been expected to contemplate.

The keystone of the art of the community trust remains the perpetual vigilance to "change with change," the heart of Mr. Goff's model. The "dead hand" is still the enemy to be met and vanquished, but in the fifty years, due to the most astonishing violence and velocity of change the world ever has seen, some other idealisms have grown up to stand shoulder to shoulder with the original driving inspiration. Every foundation today faces up to obligation and opportunity for human relief and betterment of which the times of fifty years ago could have managed no real comprehension. Social faiths and standards of fifty years ago have been replaced, reorganized, revolutionized, and revised upwards; the armies of supporters, with new banners, have responded by a mighty growth in numbers, conviction, and effectiveness. Pondering these fifty years, Ralph Hayes recently wrote:

"At the century's turn, a stable universe revolved around an ordered earth, with resources seemingly inexhaustible and continuity apparently indestructible. The past was secure, the future unchallenged . . . Then the roof fell in; the tranquil planet that our fathers knew was wrecked. Convulsed by hot and cold wars . . . the titanic confrontation of East and West . . . man was flung into orbit in a cosmos he never made and only dimly knew. Even if survival is achieved, a recapture of security and serenity may tax the capacities of generations. Much of the burden involved will fall to official agencies, but all the support that private sources can summon will not exceed the needs. If in this turbulence, social institutions can find new nourishment in the rising resources of the community trusts, these will have creditably served their founders."

One thinks of those early years during which Mr. Goff and his pioneer colleagues around the country became so impatient that the new form for philanthropic insurance did not grow, was not appreciated, more rapidly. But every clue to their hopes and expectations of that day indicates that they could never have perceived the magnitude and sweep of community trust dimensions of today. Certainly not the broad uses of philanthropy, a mere half century later, as foundations have discovered and developed them; probably not the ever-increasing race of givers to support ever-increasing social benefits. It has been a great idea, that of protecting good works through the unforeseeable future of changing wisdoms. How well it is doing summons up one of those rare intimations that humanity, once in a while, takes a whole stride in the direction of that millennium of perfections of which we dream.

ABOUT THE AUTHOR

IN THE BEGINNING this was a book in search of an author.

Fortunately — for the Cleveland Foundation and the reader alike — the search was brief and the author superbly qualified.

As the editor-in-chief of the *Cleveland News for* 23 years, and before that as reporter, city editor, and managing editor of the *Cleveland Plain Dealer* (to which he still contributes editorially), Nat Howard has had much to say over the years about the Foundation's efforts and progress.

As a reporter he covered such stories as the Foundation's Survey on Criminal Justice, which brought about badly needed reforms that halted a series of crime waves in the city and set a precedent that was to be followed by other major cities in the nation. He has seen fit over the years to write numerous editorials about the Foundation — editorials backed by a thorough working knowledge of the Foundation's aims, the city's needs and the interrelation of the two. His knowledge of the city's political scene (not to mention the nation's) and of the people who have helped make Cleveland what it is approaches the encyclopedic.

Howard's scope is not limited to the local scene. In World War II he headed the department of press censorship in Washington. In 1948 he served as president of the American Society of Newspaper Editors, and for eight years was a director of the Associated Press.

INDEX

Bohm, Katherine Fund • 66
Bole, Mrs. Benjamin P. • 67
Boston Committee of the Permanent Charity Fund • 37, 39, 42, 45-46, 72, 74, 80-82, 89, 90, 96
Boston Light • 73
Boston Opera Association • 81
Boston Safe Deposit & Trust Co. • 42, 45, 81
Boston United Fund • 81
Boyd, George H. Fund • 63
Boynton, Nap. H. • 67
Brand, Carl W. • 67
Brooklyn Institute of Arts and Sciences • 50
Brown, James IV • 55, 78
Brown, John Mason • 75
Buffalo Foundation • 38, 52, 69, 72, 95-96
Burns, Allen T. • 16-17, 21, 24-25
Burroughs, Charles F. • 93
Butler, Mr. and Mrs. Burridge D. • 79

Calgary Foundation • 73
California Community Foundation • 37, 72
Cambridge Foundation • 37
Carnegie, Andrew • 13
Carnegie Foundation • 24, 25
Carnegie Institute • 13
Carter, Leyton E. • 49, 55, 61, 69
Case Institute of Technology • 69
Center on Alcoholism (Cleveland) • 59
Central National Bank (Cleveland) • 60, 68
Central United Bank (Cleveland) • 34
Chamber of Commerce (U.S.) • 69
Chapin, Fred H. • 67
Chapin, Fred H. Memorial Fund • 62, 63, 66
Chauncy Hall School • 81
Chicago Community Chest • 95
Chicago Community Fund • 45
Chicago Community Trust • 37, 39, 41, 43-45, 72, 78, 88, 90, 91, 95
Chicago Convalescent Home for Women and Children • 80
Chicago Rotary Clubs • 45
Chicago, University of • 16
Chicago Veterans' Administration Hospitals • 45
Clark, Mr. and Mrs. Harold T. • 60, 67
Cleveland Automobile Club • 27
Cleveland Bar Association • 27-29
Cleveland Chamber of Commerce • 28
Cleveland Commission on Higher Education • 59